Here's what people are saying about *Burdens Do a Body Good:*

Burdens Do a Body Good . . . such an intriguing title for a terrific read! Packed with insight, perspective, and clear-cut strategies, Michele and Dr. Foetisch's book is a roadmap to navigate through the twists and turns life offers, good and bad; for not just surviving, but thriving.

Maria Bailey, author, talk show host for Lifetime, and host of Mom Talk Radio

Michele writes in a style that is woman to woman, it feels so personal, and yet at the same time draws her reader in to a larger community of women in which she tackles challenges we all face. In reading this book I felt understood, supported, empowered by knowledge, inspired by practical advice and spiritual insight, and held graciously accountable to be changed by what I was learning.

Sarah Zacharias Davis, author of *The Friends We Keep*

This unique blend of Michele Howe's compassionate reflections on difficult circumstances and Dr. Foetisch's practical advice on dealing with stress, illness, and injury will help many Christian women cope with setbacks. Whether you're facing situational life challenges such as divorce or job loss, or more systemic difficulties such as disappointment and doubt, this inspirational guide demonstrates both spiritual and medical ways to keep putting one foot in front of the other.

Jana Riess, author of *What Would Buffy Do?* and *American Pilgrimage*

Michele Howe and Christopher Foetisch, MD, have written an absolutely beautiful and inspiring book about overcoming obstacles, moving on, and creating value out of any circumstance.

Jonny Bowden, PhD, CNS, author of *The Most Effective Ways to Live Longer*

As a surgeon, I'm a bottom-liner. I want practical, not ethereal, but at the same time, as a Christian, I want sound Biblical advice, not feel-good pop psychology. Now you know why I like this book! Get out your highlighter; you're going to want to go back to your favorite sections over and over when you find yourself up against life's burdens.

Harry Kraus, MD, best-selling author of *Domesticated Jesus*

Michele Howe and Dr. Christopher Foetisch offer great advice for women to optimize their physical, mental, emotional, and spiritual health. Th "ck-bite-size" servings are perfect for the bus

Rick Johnson, best-selling author of *The l*
Spouse's Better Half

Inspiring and informative, *Burdens Do a Body Good* will challenge you to reconsider your definition of true health. It's the perfect book for any woman who needs a generous dose of both grace and grit!

Ginger Garrett, author of *Beauty Secrets of the Bible*

Every day we are asked to do more and accomplish it faster, multitasking if possible. It is vital that we learn to be gentle with ourselves. That's why I like this book, *Burdens Do a Body Good*. The authors, Michele Howe and Dr. Christopher Foetisch, don't add more to our plate. They walk alongside us with heartfelt and pragmatic wisdom about real challenges and give us the permission to embrace the resources that are already within.

Terry Hershey, author of *The Power of Pause*

In *Burdens Do a Body Good*, talented author Michele Howe and noted orthopedic surgeon Dr. Christopher A. Foetisch team up to give women a resource for those moments when life seems to be spinning out of control. Advice on dealing with a wide range of physical and emotional challenges is delivered in manner that is always accessible, practical, and inspirational. Give this book to a friend who is going through a difficult time in her life, or give yourself the uplifting gift of Michele and Dr. Foetisch's companionship and encouragement along each day's winding path. Their words will help you transcend some of life's greatest challenges with positivity and good health.

Lisa Hendey, founder of CatholicMom.com and author of *The Handbook for Catholic Moms*

Burdens Do a Body Good is fabulously written! This book is a paradigm shifter, possessing the power to lift women's perspective above the common pitfalls of physical, emotional, and mental setbacks while providing expert solutions and doable actions for a more healthy and productive life! Read and change your perspective on how to overcome the challenges of fear, depression, failure, and relational difficulties!

Coach Anna McCoy, author and founder of Woman, Act Now

Inspirational and self-help books flood the market. Rarely does one discover a work of art that stirs the soul like *Burdens Do a Body Good*. There is a unique style, a combination of spiritual depth and practical direction that put this book in a class of its own. Michele and Dr. Foetisch's book is sure to encourage a life-transforming journey to its readers.

Lisa Marie Samaha, DDS

BURDENS DO A BODY GOOD

BURDENS DO A BODY GOOD

Meeting Life's Challenges
with Strength (and Soul)

Michele Howe and
Dr. Christopher A. Foetisch

HENDRICKSON
PUBLISHERS

Burdens Do a Body Good: Meeting Life's Challenges with Strength (and Soul)
© 2010 by Hendrickson Publishers Marketing, LLC
P.O. Box 3473
Peabody, Massachusetts 01961-3473

ISBN 978-1-59856-433-4

Printed in the United States of America

First Printing — May 2010

Hendrickson Publishers is strongly committed to environmentally responsible printing practices. The pages of this book were printed on 30% post consumer waste recycled stock using only soy or vegetable content inks.

Author photo by Alison Ross with Ali Anne Photography. Used with permission.

Library of Congress Cataloging-in-Publication Data

Howe, Michele.
    Burdens do a body good : meeting life's challenges with
strength (and soul) / Michele Howe and Christopher A. Foetisch.
      p. cm.
   ISBN 978-1-59856-433-4 (alk. paper)
    1. Life change events. 2. Women—Conduct of life. 3. Resilience
(Personality trait) I. Foetisch, Christopher A., 1965– II. Title.
    BF637.L53H69 2010
    155.3′33—dc22
                        2010004514

Dedications

Michele would like to thank her husband Jim for giving her room to write, with gratitude.

And her children,
Nicole (and Jimmy)
Katlyn (and Chase)
Corinne
Jamey

(You have each other's backs in good times and bad . . . that alone brings joy to my heart.)

Dr. Foetisch would like to thank his wife Chris, his son Jack, and his daughter Kylie for their love and support.

☙ Table of Contents ☙

Table of Contents

❧ ACKNOWLEDGMENTS ❧

Life has a way of nudging us into new directions, new places, and amongst new people (often whether we like it or not). So, it's a truly wonderful experience when we can choose those with whom to share part of the journey. From start to finish, it's been our pleasure to work together with the always first-rate editorial team at Hendrickson Publishers.

Michele and Dr. Foetisch would like to especially thank Hendrickson's editorial director, Shirley Decker-Lucke, for seeing the value of pairing inspirational stories with practical women's health recommendations. Shirley, as a woman and as a publishing professional, understands the countless ways today's women are being challenged across every area of life. This book answers that felt need.

To Kathy Russ and Megan Talbot . . . we appreciate your timely responses to every request, be it of the marketing or administrative sort. You both have a knack for making our day a better one.

Our sincerest gratitude also goes to the entire Hendrickson design and sales team. Your expertise speaks for itself and you make our project a standout.

And thanks to Linda Triemstra Cook for her editorial input on fine-tuning our work to make it a better, more useful resource.

Michele and Dr. Foetisch also want to express appreciation to our agent, Les Stobbe, who makes it his business to match the right idea with the right publisher. You did it again, Les!

Finally, the authors would like to say a heartfelt thank you to the staff at The Toledo Clinic where Dr. Foetisch has his medical practice. To office manager, Mandi Randall, thanks of the super-sized kind for happily scheduling and re-scheduling on our behalf (we couldn't have done it without you). And to the rest of Dr. Foetisch's excellent team; Lori Miller, Nichole Pickett, Ryan Roth, and Jackie Skiver, your contributions are always appreciated and gratefully noted.

ॐ INTRODUCTION ॐ

It occurs to me that often when I have something on my mind, some pressing matter or concern that won't be brushed aside or hushed away, I will invariably run across something in written form on the same subject again and again and again. Finally, I get the message. It isn't always the message I want; rather, the one I need.

During the writing of this book, I encountered the same scenario. Time after time, or more accurately, page after page, I would read about women facing an insurmountable obstacle. Some were primarily emotional in scope, such as enduring long stretches of waiting or feeling hopeless, discouraged, or depressed about broken dreams or failed endeavors. Other women were fighting against the temptation to give up as exhaustion and uncertainty dogged their steps.

Then there were the other stories, those that were more experiential in nature. There are countless women who are simultaneously parenting their own children while transitioning into the dicey role of parenting their elderly moms and dads. Some are adjusting to a job relocation or job loss. Financial stresses, physical illness, and relational struggles with family, friends, and colleagues are common refrains as well. Toss aging and retirement planning into the mix, and just about everyone is contending with circumstances that are hard and appear to multiply in occurrence and intensity as time edges forward.

These stories always intrigue me, not that my situations are always so harrowing, but, comparatively so, I feel like all these other women who are facing down their private mountains. In that, I believe all women are the same . . . on the inside. We wrestle with ongoing internal dialogue, and then we wrestle over what action to take to quiet and calm those same inner voices. Most of the women I know want to make things right or at least better and spend the bulk of their lives making the attempt.

The road frequently seems so steep, so unconquerable. Oftentimes, I wonder how I'll have the strength to keep going, how I'll manage to continue facing a particularly difficult situation that doesn't appear to be going away anytime soon. Then I think about other women and how they manage to overcome whatever it is they're up against. As I pay closer attention, a certain theme emerges from these women and how they face down whatever obstacle is confronting them. There is a sure and certain need for courage and strength and a sense of fearlessness. As author Carolyn Custis James writes, "In this broken world being a woman often means doing hard things, straining your muscles, and tackling messy problems that aren't listed in books about true femininity and may actually be repudiated by them." I like this. I agree with this. Most of the women I know are living out this reality.

For this reason alone, I'm pleased to have the opportunity to offer women some resources of both the inspirational and practical sort throughout the pages of this book. I appreciate being encouraged and uplifted, but good words don't get me very far or mean very much if I don't match them with purposeful action steps. This is why women not only will be encouraged to look at many of life's weightier issues from a fresh emotional perspective but also will get powerfully effective recommendations from my co-author, Dr. Christopher A. Foetisch, an orthopedic surgeon who specializes in sports medicine.

At the close of every chapter, Dr. Foetisch offers valuable information and insights on staying strong, living at your healthiest best, and making sure you stay that way no matter what your age. You will be delighted and surprised at the recommendations, choices, and options available to you. It is our hope that you, our readers, can discover new ways of dealing with old problems, that every woman will be better fitted to embrace courageous perspectives, gain renewed strength, and exhibit a good measure of fearlessness for all of life's challenges, be they emotional or situational or both.

❧ Part 1 ❧

PERSONAL LIFE CHALLENGES

1

∂ WAITING ≪
Choosing Calm Over
Control

According to my ability and judgment;
I will keep them from harm and injustice.
Hippocrates

What type of client, customer, or patient are you? When you walk through the waiting room door, does the person on the other side flinch, tense, or otherwise prepare for attack? Do you disappoint, discourage, or offer a disgruntled impression? Is every statement or question voiced one punctuated by an undergirding of subtle disrespect, disinterest, or distrust? What is your attitude saying about you, your words notwithstanding?

It used to be that physicians had to memorize the Hippocratic oath, the most memorable line, to laypeople, being, "First, do no harm." Nowadays, this pledge has been updated to reflect a modern, high-tech society. Still, the underlying message remains the same. That is, one individual is making a promise to do his or her level best to help another person in need. Honestly now, aren't we thankful that the majority of doctors and other professionals from whom we seek aid do abide by this long-standing motto? If we didn't trust that person sitting on the other side of the desk or across the room to make a positive difference in our lives, we wouldn't waste time seeking out his or her expertise, right?

Though we continue to seek expert help from these professionals, we've similarly begun to tote along with us an attitude of consumer elitism. Truth to tell, we're ever ready to assert our rights even when they're not being compromised. We get angry when our appointment is pushed back. We feel frustrated when a promised contract doesn't materialize. We complain and fret and moan about every little inconvenience without taking time to consider that our minor grievance could transform into another's good. How is this so?

Consider this. The next time you're left waiting for an hour because of an unexpected emergency and your friendly neighborhood professional begs your pardon upon greeting you . . . give it. Think about how you feel when your best-laid plans go wrong. We've all had those days when we started out on time armed with a solid plan of great intent and then were interrupted, stalled, and thwarted. How did we feel? We were discouraged, weary, and wanted to give up. In the coming days, do yourself and everyone else a favor. Hone that memory of yours that never forgets an offense against you for the good of someone else, and take the oath to keep others from harm. Purpose never to rattle someone's already fragile emotional cage with your unrelenting demands or unrealistic expectations. Rather, tell the person that you understand. Tell them you appreciate their diligent service. Tell them thank you. You'll begin to see the person behind the professional façade, and we all know how terrific it feels to have someone see the "us" behind what we do. It can't do any harm.

Takeaway Action Thought: Never view waiting as wasted time. These are opportune moments allotted for the purpose of regaining some inner stillness, calm, and clarity.

Weight-Bearing Exercises

There are only two ways to wait. We choose either to wait well or to wait poorly. If we give in to impatient thoughts and words, then we risk jeopardizing our health and that of those with whom we come into contact. In a society in which there is only stop and go, waiting offers a welcome in-between space to purposefully hit the pause button and to rest and reflect. It doesn't matter what we're waiting for: an appointment, an apology, or an answer. It's the conduct of our heart and minds that will make all the difference.

Waiting Well

- ᔆ lowers blood pressure; when we accept the uncontrollable as necessarily part of daily life, our physical bodies take note and respond accordingly.

- ᔆ reduces inner stress; from headaches to body aches, we feel better when we realize we are not in control of others' behaviors or responses, only our own.

- ᔆ makes one more productive; being forced to wait in one area allows more time and energy to invest in countless others. There is no wasted time if we use each day to its fullest.

- ᔆ allows for better decision making; rather than reacting with anger and impulsivity, we thoughtfully consider, decide, and determine taking into account all possible repercussions of our choices.

- ᔆ expands our understanding of another's perspective; removing ourselves from the emotional intensity of the moment enables us to see a situation more accurately as time passes.

- ᔆ gives opportunity to love sacrificially; we deepen, grow, and change every time we put someone's needs above our own, personal discomfort and all.

Waiting Poorly

- ❧ raises blood pressure; as our mind thinks, our emotions flare, and from head to toe our bodies respond to the stress. What and how we process our thoughts and experiences does matter.

- ❧ produces anxiety; we fret, worry, and stew . . . and forfeit the inner peace for which we long.

- ❧ inhibits productivity; when we focus exclusively on what we can't have, we become immobilized, unable to be of any good to anyone or anything else in our lives.

- ❧ increases chances of reacting impulsively; stand back, don't react. The more frequently a person acts or speaks before thinking, the greater the potential for negative and long-lasting fallout.

- ❧ shrinks one's sense of proportion; when we see only our side of a situation, we're not viewing life as it is. Whenever there are two people, there are two sides to every story, always.

- ❧ robs us of our ability to grow by enduring difficulties; when we respond self-protectively or solely with self-interest, we are the ones who are short-changed most.

❧❧❧❧

Wait for the LORD; be strong and take heart and wait for the LORD.
Psalm 27:14

2

ॐ UNCERTAINTY ॐ
Defuse Your Anxiety by
Looking Out for Others

> To deeply understand fear we must also look
> at ourselves and the way we interpret our
> situations. Those scary objects can reveal
> what we cherish. They point out our insatiable
> quest for control, our sense of aloneness.
> Edward T. Welch in *Running Scared*

It hadn't been five minutes into the film "The Pursuit of Happyness" before I felt something deep inside of me rebel. That foreshadowing device found in excellent literature that honors English students are so familiar with as they learn to identify, separate out, and even anticipate was haunting me from the outset. It didn't matter that I was already aware of the storyline and the satisfactory conclusion of this particular based-on-real-life tale. It still affected me, troubled me.

I couldn't shake that insistent voice inside my head that kept saying, "This is wrong, wrong, wrong." Throughout this film, in which a family was rendered homeless after a job loss, it felt obscene that it could happen in a country like ours. And yet, seeing it on the big screen ignited something that I've had a hard time shaking. I realized that every one of us is just a few steps from some sort of life-altering catastrophe. Your potential pitfall might be a minor illness turned terminal. Another person might suffer job loss or career replacement. Someone else might lose a spouse or child to violence. The neighbor down the road, or in the next apartment, could lose her home. You see, it doesn't matter how the displacement happens or even what form it takes. The bottom line is that every man, woman, and child needs back-up, lots of back-up.

This entity we term back-up finds its form through family, friends, or work colleagues who can be counted on to lend a hand during those spaces of time when everything we've got is not enough. Think of offering the warm hand of friendship, offering forgiveness, offering whatever it is that someone you know needs as smart investment and not in the predatory, I'm-giving-to-get sense. Rather, see people's needs, really see them. Then don't go home and fret and worry and stew about it. Put feet to your newly acquired vision, and set your hands to bringing some relief, some measure of good, where it's most needed.

Whether or not you ever envision yourself as a person in need, the potential is always there. The problem is; ignoring it doesn't make the risk go away, and the time will come when you're at the mercy of others. Does that frighten you? Maybe it should. It can be a terrifying reality given some people's propensity to blindness when it comes to lending aid. Seeing is believing. We need to open our eyes and our hearts. This might equate to giving until it hurts, in our bank accounts, our time, and our talents . . . our treasures. Today, look around and willingly take on the role of being a back-up person for someone in need. Maybe in time, that fortunate soul will have your back when you require it.

Takeaway Action Thought: Oftentimes the best remedy to combat anxious uncertainty is to become another's back-up person.

Weight-Bearing Exercises

All sorts of remedies are being offered for dealing with those sudden, intense rushes of anxiety and those inner tugs to bolt from an uncertain situation. Truth is, for as many real risks as there are to our safety, there are countless more that hover threateningly within our thoughts. We might mentally understand that our fears are just that . . . fears founded in the uncertainty of life. Before we realize it, one undisciplined morsel of fear feeds on another and yet another until we are immobilized by what-ifs. Our bodies can kick into an automatic cycle of panic that stops us from thinking rationally. The next time your body has a mind of its own and begins to react in panic, give these exercises a try.

- ๛ Take several deep breaths. Inhale slowly through your nose; exhale through your mouth. Repeat.

- ๛ Focus on tightening and then relaxing one body part at a time. Methodically, work through your entire body head to toe.

- ๛ Stand up and bend over at the waist. One vertebra at a time, slowly work up to a standing position. Repeat as needed.

- ๛ Self-massage your temples and neck using firm circular motions until you feel the tension disappear.

๛๛๛๛

God is our refuge and strength, an ever-present help in trouble. Therefore we will not fear, though the earth give way and the mountains fall into the heart of the sea.
Psalm 46:1–2

3

❧ DISCOURAGEMENT ❧
Identifying Obstacles
and Implementing
Solutions

> When we are broken, angry, and grieving,
> we pour out our honest heart cries to God.
> We beg; we complain; we cry; we pout; we
> bargain; we judge; we ask for vengeance;
> we tell him life isn't fair; we suggest who
> should be hurting instead of us . . .
> Sharon Marshall in *Take My Hand*

As one season ushers in the next with those subtle yet promising first climate shifts, so can inner change begin to move and alter without us being aware. Then, without warning, something large goes off-kilter inside of us, and we're left wondering why we feel so discouraged. So we take stock of the present, and while it may not be perfect, we notice there isn't anything going on today that should trigger such low spirits. We look around and are baffled as to why our emotions are going in the opposite direction of where our mind and life are headed.

Then, we remember. The calendar does tell all if we know how to read it. Even the most cursory paging back to months or years earlier will give a woman all the insight she needs to know about why she feels discouraged. Anniversaries, good and bad, affect us today. We remember when a friend died during the heat of summer and puzzle over why we suddenly feel sad on this gloriously radiant afternoon at the beach. Or, we recall the dampness of spring that accompanied our child's lingering and unidentified illness with all its associated fears and wonder why we can't shake a sense of impending doom as spring approaches. Little or large, anything can serve as a catalyst to set off a response of seasonal discouragement, not to be confused with seasonal affective disorder. This form of discouragement can hit fall, winter, spring, or summer.

If ever a deluge of inexplicable emotional swings catches us, remembering where we were a year previous (or even ten) can offer mighty built-in relief and comfort. Suddenly, the doldrums make perfect sense, and our relief abounds. There is only one problem with this single-sided remedy: the longer women live, and the more seasonal distress events accrue over time, before we realize it, *every* season has residual and lingering afterpains. Does this mean that discouragement is given license to linger and take up residence in ever-increasing quantity? Never. While women now have more understanding about why we feel particularly sensitive during a certain time of the year, we're also forewarned to take on our discouragement more fully armed.

How is this so? It is essential that women accept the fact that feeling downhearted after any type of loss is the appropriate response to pain. Emotions are part of being human, and our responses to feeling hurt are fitting ones. The pain matters, as does its attending emotional response. However, staying at that place where discouragement reigns is wrong and cowardly. It is ever so.

Given that everyone experiences seasons of dejection, it doesn't suit for women to walk through life in a continual state of despondency. Rather, women must choose discouragement's opposite response. They must take courage. Despite how women feel, choices must continue to be made that will serve as those crucial forging instruments to rebuild our emotional structure. Like every skill, practicing courage, even emotional courage, takes deliberation, effort, and careful thought.

There is no glory or good in nursing a negative, can't-do posture. Instead, we face what's happened, accept life's ever-altering panorama, count the costs, and then rebuild with the soul of a visionary.

Author Sharon Marshall offered this pictorial vignette describing her own long season of discouragement after the death of her son and how she proceeded through it. "When hurricanes wrack the eastern seashore, the towns in the path board up. Residents plan to wait out the storm, then get on with the business of rebuilding. There are times in our lives when we need to do that. Wait out the storm. Cry our tears. Do whatever's next. Let people in to love and help us. Then when the storm subsides, begin to rebuild." For rebuild we must.

Takeaway Action Thought: Despite the bleakest circumstances, we alone retain the power to choose our response and to enact the best solution to remedy it.

Weight-Bearing Exercises

Pep talks are one of life's bonuses. Whenever we feel low, the right, good words from a friend can do wonders. Though our circumstances haven't changed, we feel differently about the situation. Often, we just feel different: better, stronger, more competent and able. We now have the courage to persist past those discouraging difficulties and see both our obstacles and

17

their corresponding solutions with greater clarity. Read on to discover what you can do if you're feeling discouraged about some aspect of a physical recovery.

∞ **Obstacle:** Sometimes people get discouraged when they've been hurting for a long time, and the recovery process now adds more time to this hard season.

Solution: Once the physical issue is addressed and corrected, the cure or fix is simpler than people realize, and given time, it will resolve itself. Adequate time is the cure.

∞ **Obstacle:** People not only have physical pain to cope with; they are dealing with other, secondary life issues that exacerbate their bodily pain from emotional and physical perspectives.

Solution: These individuals have to understand how the two problem sources have combined to create a seemingly overwhelming situation. When people see this connection and identify both parts, neither one weighs so heavily. Understanding the season is the cure.

∞ **Obstacle:** People want someone else to make it all better for them.

Solution: Individuals have to take ownership for making healthy, healing choices and need to understand there is only so much others can offer them. Accepting that no one else can take away their discouragement for them is the cure.

Why are you downcast, O my soul? Why so
disturbed within me? Put your hope in God, for I
will yet praise him, my Savior and my God.
Psalm 42:5–6

18

4

ஒ LOSS ஓ
Deciding What's Worth Losing and What's Worth Keeping

> Life comes to women in stiff doses. When it does, and we are crushed or shattered or stretched beyond our limits, we need to surround ourselves with good theologians. But at the end of the day, it won't be their theology we will lean on . . . We will lean on our own.
> Carolyn Custis James in *When Life and Beliefs Collide*

It doesn't take a workout of much mental exertion to grasp that there is a strong connection between how we view life's losses, what we believe about said life losses, and the response we subsequently offer in answer to those beliefs. There's a term for this mental gymnastic exercise that parallels life and loss, and the utterance of it can initiate a shuttering repulsion in the most stalwart of women—but it shouldn't. This thought-provoking process of reconciling what should be versus what is is what women do for our survival and for the well-being and benefit of those we love. Its proper term is "theology." Carolyn

Custis James writes, "The moment the word *why* crosses our lips, we are doing theology."

Given that definition, have you done theology today? Like it or not, if "why" has passed your lips, the answer is yes. Even though you may not name it in such eloquent terms, when a woman responds to any act of malevolence with an inner felt sense of injustice and wonders how such wrong can prevail, she is doing theology. In other words, every time a loss is tallied and the wrong side wins, we are at a crossroads of sorts. What we believe in, whether it is God or another principle of systematic belief, must be squared with hard facts. This is no easy task. It is uncomfortable. It takes energy. It takes courage. And it is a daily wrestling match of no little effort.

The fact is, no matter what women call this grappling through the enigmas of life, with all its associated suffering, and how we make our belief system fit (even to the smallest degree) is the definition of theology. Every discomfort we confront forces us to decide what we believe about life and how we reconcile the irreconcilable. In order to fully live and not merely function, we must live beyond the scope of our experiences. There has to be something sturdier, more robust, more worthy than the sum of our losses or gains and beyond our understanding. Otherwise, when the tolls begin to add up, we've nothing to lean into that's going to carry us through when life doesn't make sense.

No matter when we've experienced them, no matter what form they arrive packaged in, and no matter how frequently we've faced them down, every person, knowingly or not, wears these painful repercussions like a second skin. We feel losses, guard them, hide them, and often wouldn't know what to do without them. We'll do anything but face them, but only for so long.

Willingly or no, every person comes to that place where life becomes uncomfortable enough that he or she starts doing theology in head and heart. At this place of engagement, women cannot dismiss, excuse, or deny the truth that life and loss are twin companions; they always have been and always will be. Yet, every loss, no matter how crushing, can in time offer women something of which the world has great need.

Once women understand that as life progresses we will have to grow more comfortable with the discomfort, we will find our theology spills out into life in beautiful ways. For "true theology moves from head to heart to life." Losses, rightly understood, equip us. They set feet to once-feeble good intentions, and they strengthen women to think, reason, and then act rightly. Theology is good for women. Even when it can't right every wrong, it does its own right-side-out work where it matters most . . . inside the heart of all of us.

Takeaway Action Thought: You alone decide whether your losses will make or break you.

Weight-Bearing Exercises

Every woman understands what losing something feels like. Similarly, every woman wishes she could lose something, maybe even multiple somethings. Women know that some losses are in reality gains, like losing a bad attitude perhaps, making comparisons to others, persistent negativity, memories of hard days. There are some habits a woman is better off discarding, but when it comes to health concerns, loss normally isn't a good thing. Women have to be their own advocates for staying strong as they age. Below are some suggestions for preventing loss where it counts most.

🍃 **Loss prevention truth:** From an orthopedic surgeon's perspective, the aging process can be very unkind to females, as the issues are often insidious in nature until a big problem occurs.

🍃 **Practice prevention 1:** Osteoporosis is perhaps the least treated and yet most preventable condition. Bone loss paired with aging can produce a devastating combination; resulting in fractures and chronic pain. Significantly lower this risk by taking calcium and vitamin D supplements along with regular exercise. Routine bone density testing is also recommended to identify those who are at risk and require more aggressive treatment.

🍃 **Practice prevention 2:** Loss of muscle mass and strength, as well as reduced flexibility, is yet another risk area. This results in decreased mobility and function. Routine stretching and a simple exercise program can help dramatically.

🍃 **Practice prevention 3:** Senses begin to lose their sharpness as women age into the seventies and beyond. Hearing, taste, smell, vision, and touch may decline significantly. This loss frequently compromises appetite and diet, which directly affects nutrition and overall health. As these changes occur, awareness is key, so that an individual's diet can be modified to ensure proper nutrition.

꙳꙳꙳꙳

How long, O LORD? Will you forget me forever? How long will
you hide your face from me? How long must I wrestle with
my thoughts and every day have sorrow in my heart?
Psalm 13:1–2

5

---

૭ Depression ૭
Evaluate, Then Make Changes

Life before God is an ongoing sequence of living, evaluating, and changing, then re-evaluating and changing, then re-evaluating and changing. Depression too is an occasion for re-evaluating and changing.
Edward T. Welch in
Depression: A Stubborn Darkness

Though she didn't exactly remember what it felt like, this enigmatic condition named depression, there were reminders. The haunted look on a woman's face, or the flat sound of a hopeless voice over the phone . . . breaking apart . . . on the inside. Tears, it seemed, were an optional response, depending on how far along she was in the journey.

Tears or no, depression remained that black-ink, devoid-of-hope zone. Every time she encountered someone who was in the throes of it, her immediate impulse was to enfold that suffering soul with an embrace that promised to make it all go away. Of course, *that* was impossible. For even under the watchful care of another, powerful as that type of faithful love is, it is not potent enough to erase the depth of pain that travels entwined with depression.

No, depression has to be worked through on one's own. There is no running from it and no skirting around it. In this case, *through* is the operative word. Depression has to be pilgrimaged through to the other side, not ignored, passed by, suppressed, or denied. But can it be battled? Yes, and engaged on a variety of fronts and in a multitude of ways. For most people, this working through is endured over seemingly interminable seasons. It is a long haul of small yet significant choices that choose life in spite of the chasm of dead emotions.

Perhaps one of the most important offensive measures to enlist in a fight against this formidable foe called depression is to understand its causes. For some people, profound anger and sadness can result in depression. For others, strictly physical explanations offer some understanding why a person can feel fine one day and wake up blindsided and immobilized the next. Understanding, then, is essential, as is evaluating.

While it's true there is always an element of mystery to depression and its lingering aftereffects, frequently a careful look at one's recent medical history provides enough clues to solve the puzzle and offer small measures of consolation. Author and counselor Edward Welch encourages depression sufferers to review some common medical problems that have known depressing effects. These conditions include Parkinson's disease, strokes, multiple sclerosis, epilepsy, head trauma, lupus (SLE), vitamin deficiencies, postsurgical changes, AIDS, hepatitis, postpartum changes, hyperthyroidism, hypothyroidism, Cushing's disease, premenstrual depression, viral or bacterial infections, certain types of headaches, heart disease, side effects of medication, and chronic fatigue, as well as any chronic illness.

Understanding the possible causes of depression opens the way to knowledgeable evaluations of what's working and what isn't in your life. Evaluating then paves the way for making appropriate changes, including wise preventative ones. This process of evaluating and changing will produce the most lasting of changes in both body and soul. Evaluate and change today.

Takeaway Action Thought: Examine your life from every angle as you search for the underlying causes of depression; then evaluate and change.

Weight-Bearing Exercises

Have you ever considered how there are entire seasons in life when your emotions harbor an uncanny predilection toward forecasting all things dark and dreary? It's the rare person whose instinctive first response is to make a consistently positive prediction. Whether your current forecast is bright and sunny or more of the same (bleak and dismal), today's atmospheric condition is never the final reading. Our ever-shifting climate of emotions can alter by the hour, depending on many factors, both internal and external. Sometimes low swings into depression aren't solely emotional or even physical. Not surprisingly, they can be strongly affected by life circumstances, both the good and the bad. Read on to discover and forearm yourself and those you love about depression's varicolored precipitating causes and prevent a surprise first attack or a thunderous resurgence.

     ↬ **Positive life stress:** watch for the emotional withdrawals that accompany any positive life change. This includes job promotions, weddings, and vacations, for even the most coveted of life's milestones can bring on short-term depression in women. Many people don't realize how much emotional toll even these beneficial experiences can take.

❧ **Negative life stress:** accept its role in the scheme of life. Realize that family emergencies, extended caregiving responsibilities, financial upsets, unresolved relational issues, childcare dilemmas, and workplace challenges can all contribute to the onset of depression. Thus, enlisting and lending anticipated help before the next landslide of distressing events is especially crucial.

❧ **Exercise, stretch, and sleep:** women need these three essentials every day. As women age, regularity in habits and scheduling becomes primary. Discover the least resistant path to consistently exercise, eat healthily, and sleep effectively. Then make these practices a priority.

❧ **Realistic expectations:** these keep women from reacting by extremes. Striving for excellence is exemplary, but expecting perfection is counterproductive. It is the wise woman who does what she can to make a positive difference, understands she cannot fix every thing, person, or situation, and makes peace with that fact.

❧ **Healthy relationships:** these protect you and your health. Prudent women understand the healthiest relationships are characterized by give and take. Women should surround themselves with people who support them, those who stand by with unwavering loyalty and are at the ready to offer assistance when required.

❧❧❧❧

I wait for the LORD, my soul waits, and in his word I put my hope.
Psalm 130:5

6

⊱ EXHAUSTION ⊰
Decoding Your Body's Messages and Finding a Healthy Balance

> One of life's little ironies is that some
> of our hardest times are when our
> dreams actually do come true.
> Paula Rinehart in *Better Than My Dreams*

Everyone's heard them and repeated them. They're frequently humorous or weak attempts at poignant observations concerning the quirky things people do, think, believe, and react to about the foibles of life. But women in particular seem to relish reiterating these expressions for getting the final word. Consider this slim offering of encouragement spoken after a parenting pep talk: Keep your chin up. Or, how about this admonition uttered immediately following a rousing competitive board game in which only one person can win—and knows it: Don't get a chip on your shoulder. Take those moments when one child attempts to project blame onto his sibling by offering a purposefully confusing account of the discipline-worthy act: Cut to the chase (please). Depending upon their moment-by-moment behavior, kids are considered either the apple of my eye or the bane of my existence.

As amusing as these sayings are, the truth is there often is a grain of truth in every one. Take the idiom "getting up on the wrong side of the bed," which is code for issuing the warning, don't get up grumpy and unsocial. While this phrase is commonly given in jest, there are physiological reasons for women to wake up wrong-sided, and none are laughing matters. According to Dr. Alex Strande, director of Simply Healing Clinic in Irving, California, women's moods are intensified by ever-changing hormones, which are themselves exacerbated by lifestyle and environmental stress, irregular eating habits, junk food, some pharmaceutical drugs, too much caffeine, too little exercise, and inefficient sleep.

Note in particular the lack of sleep. Women attempt to squeeze far too many hours of work into their twenty-four-hour days. In an age when we women are fulfilling our dreams and excelling equally in the home and workplace, there is real risk of imbalance occurring as we strive to accomplish it all. It is this need for balance that Dr. Strande cites as vital, because when hormone levels are off, health problems occur with increasing regularity. Some of the more recognizable health concerns women face when hormones are not in balance include depression, mood swings, anxiety, night sweats, irritability, insomnia, fatigue, mental fogginess, and weight gain. Strande tells women to take an overall view of their lives and not look for a pill to make it all go away. Medication often only masks the core problems. We must recognize it is our responsibility to be proactive in all phases of our treatment plan; this entails an intelligent exchange of information with our health care providers, doing necessary homework, and then adopting the steps that will achieve an overall higher quality of life.

A final idiomatic word of advice to spouses, children, and others foolhardy enough to comment on a sleep-deprived woman's early morning attitude, actions, or attire: Do what your mother always taught you (give her the benefit of the doubt); it may have been a rough and sleepless night indeed.

Takeaway Action Thought: Physical exhaustion is your body's way of sounding a wake-up call that you're trying to accomplish too much, too fast, too often.

Weight-Bearing Exercises

What is the most common area in which women repeatedly cut corners so as to complete daily work? Sleep. Hands down, women consistently skimp on the hours we allot for nighttime rest to stay up late enough to finish up or catch up on jobs needing doing. What we don't realize is we are eventually going to pay an even higher price than we might suppose once our bodies reach that red-alert point. Life is hectic. Demands come in quick succession, and no doubt they always will. There are new opportunities and favorable possibilities around every corner, but there's only one you, so take good care, and rest responsibly. Make it as serious a business as any professional pursuit you undertake.

꽃 **Body facts:** Sleep is the time for the body to repair and restore itself.

Life implications: When a woman doesn't get enough rest, she starts the day with a physical deficit. She feels the effect of the day's pressures more keenly and frequently finds herself relying on stimulants to push through the day's responsibilities.

⌔ **Body facts:** Sleep debt results in mental, emotional, and physical fatigue.

Life implications: The day's stresses can feel like too much to handle. A woman's ability to act decisively and with confidence is reduced. Often a woman's perceptions become skewed as well, causing her to oversensitize the events and situations she would normally dismiss or ignore.

⌔ **Body facts:** Wound healing, the immune system, and metabolism are negatively affected by lack of sleep.

Life implications: A woman is less able to kick that virus, cold, or other ailment quickly, and she might find her symptoms linger longer and even develop into more serious conditions over time.

⌔ **Body facts:** Decision making, reasoning, and memory are also directly impaired by sleep deprivation.

Life implications: The ability to creatively problem solve, make plans, and develop presentations is compromised when relying on a tired mind. A woman soon realizes that such tasks take longer and require more energy when she is sleep deprived, thus erasing the time-saving benefit she mistakenly believed her into-the-night work habits profited her.

Find rest, O my soul, in God alone; my hope comes from him.
Psalm 62:5

7

---

೨ SORROW ೦
Facing Difficult Situations with Courage, Strength, and Fearlessness

> Sorrow can go only as deep as love. And
> always, always, love is the ground beneath
> sorrow as well as the sky above it.
>
> Gregory Floyd in *A Grief Unveiled*

Life is fragile, and I can prove it. During the past few weeks, two distinctively unique experiences invaded my "life is frail" consciousness. All this came by way of a car crash and a relative's terminal illness. In the space of a few hours, I witnessed two cars smash headlong into each other like two tin cans being crushed under a malevolent foot. My heart stopped. My stomach lurched. Amazingly, no one was badly injured. These families and all who love them were spared the sudden finality of death. Fast forward to a brief but soulful conversation with my father-in-law about the day's activities: getting dressed, getting down food and medicine, getting ready for radiation treatment, getting back home for a visit from a hospice nurse, getting down more food and medicine, getting tired, getting ready for bed, and getting a good night's sleep.

It seems his days are all about getting ready. But in reality, he's already ready. He is; he's farther along in this journey of life than we are, and he knows it. He's accepted it, and he wants us to accept it too. Since we're all going to die, this isn't a revelation. And still, I wonder if any of us is prepared to lose someone we love?

For our family, we've been given notice, so to speak. Someone we love dearly isn't going to recover, is likely to suffer, and we can't fix it. When we first received the news, we were still grieving over the loss of two other family members who'd recently passed away. This newest blow hurt us deeply and set us scurrying to make sense of yet another personal loss of life. This news caused an ache so real we felt it physically.

Then time stepped in, and faith. We slowly wrapped our minds around the truth, and our emotions started to catch up with the hard facts. We still ached, and our tears spilled over at inopportune moments, embarrassing us and others who looked on helplessly.

Then we turned another corner. We accepted it. In tiny, halting steps, we slowly began to see this advance notice as a blessed gift to spend time together to talk, laugh, pray, eat, and reflect. Just being together enjoying the simplest of life's pleasures means everything now. It is a good day to be alive.

Then we began to see, really see, what's important and what's not, what lasts and what won't. And those things that fall into the "what won't last" are what we spend the bulk of our days chasing: money, careers, achievement, possessions, more money. Just stuff, really, not worth a single cent in eternity. Only God and people are forever. That's it, that's the end of the story.

Or is it? Conversations are turning more and more to the life after this one, and we've discovered in the midst of the emotional pain that a sure and certain hope is a wonderful thing. And it's real, a peace-inviting, anxiety-nixing gift straight from the hand of God. Selah . . . peace. From the inside out, may you find it today.

Takeaway Action Thought: It is not selfish to take care of you in the midst of sorrowful situations. It is necessary, and it is smart.

Weight-Bearing Exercises

During seasons of loss and sorrow, one of the first things relegated to the bottom of a woman's to-do list is self-care. While life and its accompanying emotional pain presses in on her, a woman frequently forfeits one of her strongest coping commodities, her physical and emotional well-being, by simple neglect. Women, as the givers of care, must be proactive in daily self-care in order to cope effectively and deal with the many layers of grief that come with sorrow and loss.

Emotional Courage

ℓ Face facts and do something about them. When sorrows tally up, women need to harness and guard their emotional strength.

ℓ Balance work, home, and relaxation; don't take on new responsibilities during this time.

ℓ Talk with trusted friends about what you're feeling; as you do, you'll find the weight of sorrow is shared as it is distributed some amongst people who care.

ℓ Understand your limitations; listen to what others are observing in you and heed their counsel.

Physical Strength

৯ Make sure you're fit for what's coming. When sorrow makes its presence known day after day, women need to build up and maintain their physical strength.

৯ Exercise daily; set and maintain your routine of getting a minimum of twenty minutes three times per week.

৯ Get enough sleep; factor in seven to eight hours of rest every night.

৯ Take vitamin supplements daily, and eat for optimal health to offset the extra emotional pressures.

Spiritual Fearlessness

৯ Move forward even when the outcome is uncertain. When the worst is over, women need to decide what they believe, why they believe, and how their beliefs will equip them to face the future. Here they develop their spiritual strength.

৯ Revisit and re-evaluate former belief systems. Ask yourself how what you say you believe about life, death, and suffering makes a difference.

৯ What did you learn about yourself and about how you handle loss and sorrow?

৯ Contemplate tomorrow in the aftermath of today's painful circumstance. What can you do to be better prepared for future challenges?

ᲠᲠᲠᲠ

You keep track of all my sorrows. You have collected all my tears in your bottle. You have recorded each one in your book.
Psalm 56:8 NLT

8

⮞ GIVING UP ⮜
Words That Provide
Emotional Strength to
Keep Going

> Barter: to trade by exchanging
> one commodity for another.
> *Merriam Webster's Collegiate Dictionary*

Bartering. If you're a woman, then you've done it. The very term conjures up some interesting and colorful scenes in our minds. Think back to the early days of our country's history when money was scarce; what did women do? They traded one commodity for another, one's own valued item for someone else's. Whether it was a chicken or its eggs, a cow or its milk, women instinctively understood the importance of bartering wisely and prudently. It would never do to give away one's treasures without also receiving something by way of return. If a woman was careful and conscientious, she would walk away feeling encouraged and uplifted. By day's end, both participants were recipients; more important, both were gainers.

If, however, a woman had had a specific need, be it material, emotional, or spiritual, and no one with which to make a connection for direction or for guidance, then she'd end up in dire straits. Periodically stranded, isolated, or emotionally adrift, women have found sure comfort in the company of other women. Who better to commiserate with over the silent pains of relationships gone awry? Career detours or even job elimination? Health or financial setbacks? It is here, in these common-life seasons of sorrow, where women's innate instinct to reach out shine brightest. One word of caution: a giver's mentality is a given in the world of bartering. Whatever the circumstance, bartering is the means to offering mutual constancy, strength, support, and a camaraderie that knits one female to another. As women, we live lives of intersection, and not only were we born to become experts at it, we are blessed because of it. Constructive communication is where bartering speaks best.

𝔞 Build a relationship by looking for opportunities to enter gently into another woman's world. Look for common interests, goals, or similarities. Start with simple gestures of kindness, and as trust slowly builds, allow the friendship to take on a life of its own.

𝔞 Accept others as you would like to be accepted, unconditionally. Realize that affirming another person's value doesn't equate to agreeing with all her choices.

𝔞 Respect the fact that two people will never agree on every issue. Develop an active listening mentality; be proactive in attuning yourself to truly hearing what someone else is saying. Seek to understand the struggles in her world.

𝔞 Tell friends the truth. Speak constructive words that are going somewhere, are intent on a specific purpose or outcome yet always tempered by kindness. Remember the power words wield. Never batter another woman with this tool simply to make a point.

ॐ Exercise a "what are the possibilities, not the limitations" mentality. Encourage an attitude of forward movement, and pass it on. Refuse to stagnate in a specific place, position, or circumstance. Cheer your friends to the same end.

ॐ Responsibly consider making suggestions, and offer tangible help to make changes happen, for a more healthy life spiritually, physically, and emotionally. Encourage decisions that bring life and wellness to your friend, and walk alongside her, applauding her efforts day by day.

Takeaway Action Thought: A few powerful, well-chosen words of encouragement always make more of an impact than a litany of weak ones. Choose words well.

Weight-Bearing Exercises

Every woman can remember when the temptation to give up or in to failure and lingering discouragement felt paralyzing. What every woman needs at this pivotal juncture isn't a plan, a fix-it, or a pep talk. All she needs is a friend who understands and listens without judgment, without comment, or without casting blame. There will be a time later for offering suggestions, the next step, or an alternative route. As women, we need to be tuned in enough to one another's deepest, most heartfelt needs to recognize there is a right time to lend advice and a right time to withhold it. Sometimes we barter best with the gift of presence alone.

ॐ **B: begin by listening.** Sometimes words do get in the way. Emphasize the "b" in simply being there, present and accounted for, listening without mentally working out how to offer advice.

❧ **A: assign no blame.** Mercy rises above judgment. Give it completely, absolutely, and without hesitation. Even if your friend has blundered badly, realize every one of us is only a few steps or choices away from the same position.

❧ **R: resist the urge to immediately problem solve.** Most issues of any significance do not arise overnight, and neither do their solutions. Take care, and be careful about swiftly offering remedies that may only add to the complexity of the problem.

❧ **T: take all the time that is needed.** There is no gift like the gift of being 100 percent present, with no other agendas or pressing matters vying for your attention and time. Give this gift of focused attentiveness, and let your friend know you're there for the duration.

❧ **E: encourage in a way that is seen, felt, and heard.** Be aware that little of what you say will matter as much as how you say it. Let your genuine, heartfelt care be visible through every part of your physical body. Engage your friend with the entirety of you.

❧ **R: remember we're all the same inside.** Your situation may be different from mine, but inside, where it counts, we're exactly alike. Respond to another's distress, even when you don't understand its cause, in the way you'd want to be treated after enduring your worst fear.

❧❧❧❧

You [God] stoop down to make me great. You broaden the path beneath me, so that my ankles do not turn.
Psalm 18:35–36

9

❧ HOPELESSNESS ❧
How Today's Difficulties
Equip Us for Tomorrow

Sometimes following God means throwing
caution to the wind. Sometimes caution
is a symptom of faithlessness.
Carolyn Custis James in *The Gospel of Ruth*

How often have you heard someone emphatically state, "I can't take this situation a second longer"? Or, "This is impossible. Things will never change." Or even, "This just isn't right." Or, "I can't do this anymore. I'm done." Hopelessness. You can hear it with every finely punctuated word, see it on a person's dejected face, and sense its pervasive presence reverberating through the air. And the effect of hopelessness can be just as bone-chilling to observe as it is to feel. By definition, to be hopeless is to be past remedy, incurable, beyond recall, irrevocable, irreversible, irreparable, irredeemable, and irretrievable. All around, it's awful.

The interesting thing about feeling hopeless is that it's not so much about feelings as a person might think. It's more about developing thoughtful, far-reaching perspectives and letting experience work its wonders. It's about your experience and mine and how they can fortify us for the next round, come what may.

Often, when someone says she feels hopeless, what she means is that something or someone in her life causes her great distress. She feels powerless to combat the effects this particular troubling situation or person imposes upon her. Just like habits, bad experiences die hard deaths, as do our reactions and responses to them. This is especially true if they tend to linger and make messes around the edges of our lives, infringe upon our spaces, and clutter up our otherwise tidy (so we believe) existence.

There are different kinds of hopelessness to wade through, a fact that further muddies the waters of seeing and defining life with hopeful clarity. We can and do feel hopeless for our own plight, but frequently, a more potent type of hopelessness is that stinging awareness that someone we care about faces an adversity too burdensome to carry or relieve. It is this second form that can send us headlong into bouts of hopelessness too weighty for us to handle. And after hopelessness, what's next? Standing paralyzed, far too cautious, and in no way prepared to offer comfort or relief where it's needed most.

This is exactly why women must take the initiative and courageously move into places, among people, and through situations uncomfortable to them. Throwing caution to the wind is sometimes, in response to another's cry for help and when we're feeling hopeless ourselves, the right reply to a hopeless situation. Author Carolyn Custis James offers the sort of courageous initiatives everyone hopes to receive at their lowest point. James writes, "*Hesed* (a Hebrew word encompassing, but not limited to . . . steadfast, unfailing love) is driven, not by duty or legal obligation, but by a bone-deep commitment—a loyal, selfless love that motivates a person to do voluntarily what no one has the right to expect or ask of them. They have the freedom to act or walk away without the slightest injury to their reputation. Yet they willingly pour themselves out for the good of someone else." James suggests it is our duty to courageously (faithfully) exhibit *hesed* toward those within our influence.

The next time you are tempted to give in to hopelessness in thoughts, word, or deed, remember this fact: whatever hopelessly dire situation you've already faced and survived makes you all the fitter to excel at overcoming it again . . . and again . . . and again. By duty and design, choosing to press forward in spite of a hopeless situation is where we find our courage and others find hope as receivers of our *hesed*.

Takeaway Action Thought: Tough experiences equip us to face and overcome whatever's next with a hopeful boldness we would never have gained in any other way.

Weight-Bearing Exercises

There are a lot of reasons to feel temporary hopelessness, some good reasons, some not so good. Women may one day discover they are facing a diagnosis no one wants to hear and where the road ahead is fraught with potential complications and will most certainly entail some pain. But what was once considered a hopeless case often isn't the case anymore. Great strides have been made in medicine, and today's physicians have more to offer their patients than ever before. There is reason to hope! Read on and be encouraged.

∾ **Hopeless:** In orthopedic surgery, advances happen routinely. Physicians in this field regularly see a large number of women with rotator cuff tears. Many of these patients have large tears that are not repairable. In the past, the treatment was that of benign neglect (watching a problem clinically but not treating it). Often, an individual would have to endure chronic pain and have very little use and strength in the affected shoulder.

ॐ **Hopeful:** Today, however, there is an option available for a special type of shoulder replacement called a reverse total shoulder arthroplasty. This procedure is typically recommended for those over age sixty-five. The results are very good for pain relief, and overall function is improved significantly.

ॐ **More hopeful yet:** Another area that has seen dramatic advances is that of repair to cartilage damage in individuals under age forty. Several new procedures allow surgeons to repair damaged cartilage. Check with your surgeon for specific options. These procedures can delay and sometimes reduce the need for a joint replacement later in life.

ॐॐॐॐ

The LORD is my portion; therefore I will wait for him. The LORD is good to those whose hope is in him, to the one who seeks him.
Lamentations 3:24–25

10

๛ CONFINEMENT ๛
Making Decisions That Offer the Best Types of Freedom

Lifestyle diseases—what are they? Simply
put, lifestyle diseases are those diseases
caused by the way in which we live our life.
Perhaps lifestyle disease is communicable.
You catch it through prosperity.
Will Samson in *Enough: Contentment
in an Age of Excess*

From the get-go we are consumers. As babies, toddlers, and teens, all we do is consume, imbibe, and ingest. If youngsters had their way, that pattern would continue well into adulthood. So parents set their mind to train and teach their sons and daughters that life does not revolve around them. This on-going instruction is a real mercy for the children and for the world at large.

Even into adulthood, and at every opportunity, we of the consumer mindset are keenly alert to the possibilities of satisfying our senses with something that pleases us. Little do we realize that in our prosperous society our choices frequently confine, define, and serve to hinder more than benefit us.

Consumer-implied choices confine us. We are walled in by them through and through. It is via this consumerist mindset that we discover how bound we are by our endless options. Whether our preference is to select for ourselves a life characterized by the pursuit of too much leisure, the lure of materialism, constant electronic distraction, or any of the preceding combinations, our society is paying the price for such indulgences. It's not healthy to be wealthy, but we are not wise enough to see beyond the adverse effects such a consumerist mentality and subsequent affluent lifestyle offers.

For many people, the choices they made years earlier render them incapable of living freely today. The mortgage is a burden. Cars are a depreciating drain. Schooling is a nightmare. Funding for these necessities challenges even the sturdiest resolve to live more simply. Trying to calm down, quiet down, tone down all those compelling voices in our heads telling us we're missing out when we don't have it now grows increasingly more difficult over time. Waiting, or doing without, is a virtually forgotten concept, and with lives so full there's no time to contemplate important matters. Distraction can consume us as well.

Author Will Samson reminds consumerists that having so many choices, endless options, and the means to obtain them is indeed a double-edged sword that mostly works against the well-being of individuals and society alike. Certainly our blaring affluence does not benefit or meet the needs of those neighbors without similar adequate resources.

Writes Samson, "Prosperity brings privilege, and privilege—the ability to make decisions based on our individual benefit—is itself a kind of contagion." For most people, there's no stopping the flow of take, take, and take (or intake) because avid consumerists see no need to resist because of incessant, unlimited availability. There lies the problem. In not recognizing the needs and neediness of those around us, we quickly grow into self-confined, self-absorbed malcontents. This self-focus blinds us to the truth that we're all bound together, responsible for one another, and accountable to care for each other's needs above our own.

Nowhere in this self-consumed consumerist formula is there an awareness of another choice. Again, consumers have bought into the system body and soul. Rarely does an individual bail out and begin treading a different more costly path of self-denial.

Freedom from the drudgery of confining consumerism can work itself out only through simple, nondescript acts of daily life by giving, sharing, and serving. Grasping (with open hands) the less is more maxim. And it's good to remember none of it belongs to any of us anyway.

Takeaway Action Thought: If you're confined by discontent, you'll suffer the loss of freedom that contentment alone supplies.

Weight-Bearing Exercises

No one wants to be confined, whether the context be a financial, relational, or physical one. In particular, no person enjoys those stretches of time in between setting goals toward freedoms of every sort, both the internal and the external. Everyone wants to get there now, and no matter which way a person interprets it, undoing old habits and creating new healthier ones is hard work. So what should we do during that slow stretch of time that leads to eventual overall wellness and freedom? Read on to discover how to make those in-between hours and days count for something.

> **Setting the Standard:** Recognize how the culture affects and impacts every buying decision you make. From the time you get up in the morning until you lay your head down at night; you are constantly bombarded with the media's influences persuading you that no matter what your income level, your standard of living isn't enough. **Remedy:** Recognize you're not immune to society's influence.

> **At Home:** Develop a long-term plan for better financial, relational, and physical health. Look around your home and ruthlessly get rid of what you don't use. Do a mental inventory of your key relationships and honestly assess which are healthy and which are not and be willing to remove yourself from them or do the hard work of changing the dynamics. Take a look at your physical state and take the first steps toward better health by decreasing your input and increasing your output. **Remedy:** Consume less and give more across every area of your life.

> **Out and About:** With fresh eyes, purposefully look with intent to see the world around you as would a foreigner from a Third World country. Be alert to excess in its endless forms, be aware of material waste of every type, and be willing to say no to yourself, so that you can say yes to the needs of others. **Remedy:** Become the most creative (contented) consumerist you know.

రారారారా

But godliness with contentment is great gain.
1 Timothy 6:6

11

ъ REGRET ᘒ
When We Pay Attention
to the Wrong Things

> Candles seem to create peace. You don't find
> candles lit in frenetic houses; you find them lit in
> houses where people are trying to pay attention.
> Lauren Winner in *Mudhouse Sabbath*

Regrets come in all shapes and sizes, and it's safe to assume everyone has at least a few of them. Sometimes a regret is of the miniscule type: we missed an opportunity and had to wait until it presented itself again, and its worst effect was a small measure of temporary discomfort. Other regrets, however, those of the mammoth, life-altering kind, can spark a high-voltage reaction the likes of which send our pulses racing and hearts pounding, and no amount of hand wringing or floor pacing can undo the act or reduce our reaction whenever we recall it. Looking back with regrets in tow, do we ever consider what place our personal agendas had in creating such havoc? If we're honest, probably not often enough.

What were we missing? It seems that regrets occur most often and in alarmingly quick succession when people don't

47

pay attention to details, to surroundings, and to other people. And why is this? Agendas. Those pesky personal agendas zero in only on achieving their end goal. The problem with agendas is that individuals arrive with them fist-clenched and fully convinced their assumptions about a person or a situation are absolutely, infallibly correct. Given such a narrow and so fiercely self-fortified attitude, we can see how the important stuff gets passed by. It's a perfect case of majoring on the minors and subsequently missing the best part, which is a person, the moment, no regrets.

Whenever we enter a situation ready, as in armed and dangerous with a presupposed agenda, we're already missing the moment, even before it begins. We hold private conferences with ourselves and decide what's best for another person, and when given the next opportunity, we're ready to take advantage of the situation and twist it toward meeting whatever agenda we have espoused. And we miss the moment.

How long before we realize that agendas are primarily selfish ones and no manner of altruistic self-deception can change that fact? We are too given to making sure others see the same light we've seen and walk accordingly. We aim to convince, persuade, and cajole others to see our views as gospel or we agenda-nize them at first chance. Perhaps the saddest outcome of this first order of business is that we forfeit the time we're given to enjoy the people in our world. Rather than mentally positioning ourselves a few paces ahead of someone we care for, wouldn't it be far better to walk side by side, moment by moment, and let life unfold as it may?

Too much preplanning, predirecting, pre-anything spoils the moment, and people end up frustrated, aggravated, and agitated. The moment is lost. Peace is forfeited. Regrettable, isn't it?

So then, as we hone our skill in paying attention to what matters most, it should always take the preeminent position above changing others. Over and above our opinions, persuasions, and agendas, if we truly are interested in the best for someone else, we'll let our love and care and commitment speak for themselves. Remarkable, isn't it, how entering a situation freely, with no hidden agenda, results in a delightfully regret-free encounter worth the remembering?

Takeaway Action Thought: Enjoying a regret-free relationship means seeing past a person's differences and paying attention to the person.

Weight-Bearing Exercises

Timing is everything, as is paying close enough attention. Choose the wrong moment to express yourself or act, even to the right person, and things can get messy. Select the right moment to speak or do, and things generally work out nicely. The same principle holds true for choosing the appropriate time to undergo a medical procedure. It's never as simple as "getting fixed." There are a number of considerations a woman needs to pay attention to before committing herself. Read on to learn about some precautions worth contemplating so that your medical experience will be a no-regrets one.

   ↝ There is solid research indicating that if an individual is under stress, she is at an increased risk for a poor outcome after surgery. Therefore, in the case of an elective procedure, physicians may (and do) recommend delaying the surgery until circumstances have calmed down and a patient's stress level has returned to a manageable level.

❧ Another precaution a patient should take is to pose a self-examining question, "Am I having significant doubts?" This is not to be confused with the normal amount of anxiety that people generally experience prior to a surgical procedure. Rather, patients must ask themselves, "Do I feel significant apprehension and have an overwhelming concern that can't be shaken?" Some patients struggle intensely with regard to accepting the need for having the procedure done; they fear its potential outcome or are afraid of any possible complications that may occur.

❧ From the physician's standpoint, individuals need to be fully committed to proceeding with a procedure and not harbor any significant doubts before they take the next step. If a patient moves ahead despite ongoing, internal apprehension and anxiety, this fact alone is an invitation for problems to arise—and they do.

❧❧❧❧

When you [God] open your hand, they
are satisfied with good things.
Psalm 104:28

12

ও DISAPPOINTMENT ও
Putting Expectations in Their Place

> When you taste a measure of being able
> to love and enjoy the people in your life,
> without having to have any particular
> response from them, you are tasting bliss.
> Paula Rinehart in *Strong Women, Soft Hearts*

She was so disappointed with everything and everyone. She was disappointed at work, especially with those co-workers who didn't appreciate her talents and with a boss who never saw her potential and failed to promote her. She was disappointed at home, where she had kids who rarely said thank you and never picked up after themselves. Even at church, after all those years of serving faithfully, did anyone ever notice?

There she was, disappointed with her career, her family, her friendships, herself. At this point in her life, even she recognized there was no pleasing her.

"She" could be every woman. As hard as it is to admit, every woman struggles with the obvious disjoint between expectations, even the reasonable ones, and feeling undone by disappointment when said expectations don't come to pass. Somewhere in between those two realities, the one in our heads and the one that plays out in our lives, real people live. And in that reality, real people fail each other, intentionally and unintentionally.

The challenge, then, isn't to kill our hearts' desires when expectations are dashed and to allow disappointment to further bolster an already wounded heart. Instead, a reframing in the attitude department is in order. Accepting the fact that people will rarely respond in the way you might hope or think you need is a place of great freedom and peace. As one counselor puts it, always aim to weigh heavier by giving more than receiving, no matter what.

In other words, see a need; meet it. Observe a wrong; right it. Hear an unkindness; counter it. Do it with eyes that see and a heart bent on lifting the burdens of people nearest you. Do it intentionally and often. Better still, do it now.

There is a memorable line at the close of a film in which actress Diane Keaton, who portrays a woman dying of cancer, tells her younger and estranged sister that she's so grateful for the love in her life. Her sister misunderstands and assures Keaton's character that yes, everyone does indeed love her. Keaton immediately and vehemently protests and then offers clarification: "No, it's not me that's been loved." Now don't miss this important distinction. Keaton explains, "I've been blessed to have had the chance to so love *them*." So then, a met or unmet expectation can be a beautiful thing.

Takeaway Action Thought: Harness your expectations by making them work for you. Expect to see the good, and you will.

Weight-Bearing Exercises

Bad attitudes can ruin a person, top to bottom, inside and out. Negativity and all its disagreeable sidekicks will put a death knell on everything that happens between breakfast and bedtime . . . if we allow it. Those unrealistic expectations can literally eat away at us body and soul, short-circuiting the obvious good all around us. Have you ever considered how a poor outlook can even affect the healing process? Our bodies are receptacles of our entire life experience, and how we think, talk, and feel affects how effectively we heal. Part of getting better and growing stronger is being willing to do the hard work of realistically tailoring any unhealthy expectations and reframing each one so they enhance rather than detract, build rather than restore.

Reality Checks: Information You Need to Know to Heal Strong

    Elevated levels of cortisol, the body's primary stress hormone, negatively affect wound healing. High cortisol levels dampen the immune response. As a result, this imbalance can delay healing while increasing the risk for wound problems such as postsurgical infections. Similarly, stress, depression, and anxiety prior to surgery have all been linked to poor recovery after surgery.

    Any surgical procedure places an increased demand on the body. As a result, protein and calorie needs are increased by 20 to 50 percent over normal requirements. Without enough dietary protein, the body must break down muscle and organ tissue. This process can impair the immune system and deplete energy and strength needed for recovery.

    Exercise has a clearly demonstrated positive effect on surgical outcomes. According to a 2005 report from the *Journal of Gerontology*, wound healing is 25 percent faster in those patients who exercised three weeks prior to surgery compared with those who maintained their normal routine. Additionally, exercise improves circulation and strength that lead to increased mobility after surgery.

How You Think: Making Your Expectations Work for You

- ⁊ Individuals who embrace a can-do attitude and are invested in their own recovery typically do extremely well relative to those who are apprehensive or anxious prior to surgery.

- ⁊ The power of positive thinking goes a long way. Most often, if an individual thinks she will do well, she does. When a person anticipates struggling or frets about experiencing potential problems after surgery, that individual's recovery will be much tougher.

- ⁊ Adopting reasonable expectations and being willing to commit emotionally and physically to the recovery process creates the best environment for a successful outcome.

What to Do: Simple Measures to Achieve Positive Results

- ⁊ Make sure to eat a balanced diet that has adequate protein intake.

- ⁊ Exercise for a minimum of three weeks prior to surgery.

- ⁊ Avoid presurgical stress and anxiety or consider delaying an elective procedure until the intense season has passed or can be more easily managed.

In God they trusted and were not disappointed.
Psalm 22:5

13

⌥ BROKEN DREAMS ⌥
Being Tough Enough to Stay Tender

> Ours is not a culture that is comfortable with
> sadness. Sadness is awkward. It is unsettling.
> It ebbs and flows and takes its own shape. It
> beckons to be shared. It comes out in tears, and
> we don't quite know what to do with those.
> Nancy Guthrie in *Holding On to Hope*

Have you ever been sad and sorry at the same time? Maybe you've felt sad that something happened or didn't. Or perhaps you felt sorry that whatever you were hoping for isn't going to materialize as you had wanted. Have you ever found yourself wishing against all hope something had turned out differently, even just a little bit so? Every woman's been on the receiving end of a relationship, a situation, or a long-held desire that went awry. At the point of no return, that deeply imbedded moment when we realize it's over, a sad sort of relinquishment makes its presence known. We give up and walk away hoping to move past the pain and disappointment as quickly as possible. We want to forget because it hurts too much to remember and to revisit. Then we silently wonder why we made the attempt.

The problem is that we never forget. No matter how quickly we invest ourselves in a different person, situate ourselves in different surroundings, and begin formulating a different dream, we continue to carry the stinging reminders of *this* broken dream with us. There's no escaping it. Broken and bruised though we may be, there's no rushing through the residual after-effects of this present sad finale.

This is why it makes far more sense to resist the urge to turn from the pain too swiftly. We must allow the sadness and the sorrow to work within us, while it's still fresh, mind you, and before all the miserable initial hurt transcends into a different inner residue of the heart that hardens us to a point where we are brittle and embittered. To be sure, either response is going to cost us, but only the first is of the healing sort. Like it or not, when our dreams die, it's anguish.

Author Nancy Guthrie explains how her personal sorrow traversed after the death of her infant daughter. "I realized I had a choice—I could try to stuff the hurt away in a closet, pretend it wasn't there, and wish it would disappear, or I could bring it out into the open, expose it to the Light, probe it, accept it, and allow it to heal."

Tempting though it is to cease dreaming after the worst befalls us, that's no way to live. We must willingly experience the entire scope of our dreams, broken pieces and all, allowing pain to do its work, and then look expectantly ahead. Some people will insist it's not safe or prudent to dream. This is true. There is always risk. And with risk, there is discomfort . . . sometimes agonizing amounts of it.

Perhaps one of the finest results of enduring the brokenness of a dream that has died is the afterbirth of hope it carries in its wake. Despite what our traumatized hearts may tell us, the uncertainty of tomorrow can be a hopeful prospect. Not knowing what's around the next corner is a good thing indeed, even when times are hard, or especially when times are hard. There's something intrinsically hopeful about wondering, dreaming, and going for broke in pursuit of future possibilities.

Takeaway Action Thought: Don't opt out of the tougher call to stay tenderhearted after a dream dies. Be courageous enough to continue caring.

Weight-Bearing Exercises

There's an old saying, "Don't fix what isn't broken," which holds true across the lines of countless life scenarios, and yet it is during those particularly stressful seasons of life when dreams die or go amiss that women frequently forge ahead with that "fix it so they can forget it" mindset. Sometimes though, women don't even realize when something's broken or not and this holds true even in our physical bodies. Read on to better understand what the telltale signs are of real bodily broken bones.

Warnings Signals of Broken Bones

> ও Severe pain is the primary hallmark of a broken bone.

> ও The presence of deformity or significant swelling is similarly important.

> ও Difficulty using or moving the injured area in a normal manner.

> ও For a lower extremity injury, an individual will typically not be able to bear weight on a broken bone.

Helping Those Bones Heal

- ❧ While there is no quick medical remedy to make a bone heal faster, there are a variety of ways to inhibit the healing process. Topping the list of what not to do is smoking, eating poorly, and refusing to comply with your physician's instructions on follow-up care.

- ❧ Pain is the main tell-tale sign that a bone is not healing well, so take note of whether or not your level of pain is increasing or decreasing day by day.

- ❧ Always err on the side of caution. Get an x-ray because unless an obvious visual deformity is present, there is no foolproof way to be 100% percent certain a bone is not broken.

The Lord is close to the brokenhearted and
saves those crushed in spirit.
Psalm 34:18

14

❧ DOUBT ❧
Knowing Who and What to Trust

Is it possible that doubt might be one of those
unwelcome guests of life that is sometimes,
in the right circumstances, good for you?
John Ortberg in *Faith & Doubt*

Have you ever considered the upside of doubt? When you're
not certain about something or someone, you take a step back
and do some contemplating; some weighing out of the facts or
fiction presented to you. We all recognize there are times when
doubting makes plain good sense. In some circles, doubt even
has a friendlier connotation, and its name is discretion. This
ability to be discerning enough to tread carefully can offer a
woman much by way of protective buffers.

The woman who exercises a measure of discretion by
not trusting everything she's told is demonstrating both knowledge and good judgment. She's tuned in to seeing behind the
obvious and looking for telltale signs of either truth or false-
hood. But she's not a cynic, and she's rarely bitter. She's simply
honed that skill of gathering the evidence, thinking through

the objections, and weighing the consequences before moving ahead. In so doing, she's saved herself and those around her from disasters ranging anywhere from the miniscule to potentially catastrophic proportions.

There will always be room for doubt, for truly, doubt is trust's intrinsic flipside. No one fully trusts without first putting something (a belief system, a person, or a choice) through a series of mental paces. We might not consciously recognize this process, but all the same, we exercise it countless times a day. Our thoughts continually wrestle with and endure an inner give-and-take motion whenever we are presented with the unfamiliar or untested. What we conclude determines the next step, rightly so. This truism is worked out most visibly in personal relationships.

John Ortberg offers this insight into the give-and-take process that occurs daily between people in every sort of social and work situation. "When I trust you, I take a little piece of myself—my stuff, my money, my time, my heart—and put it in your hands. And then I'm vulnerable. Then you respond, and I find out whether you are trustworthy and dependable. I give you the gift of my trust, and you give me the gift of your faithfulness." It is exactly at this key juncture, in this difficult yet essential finding out that individuals make discoveries about themselves and those they've trusted. The dynamic interplay that takes place between people will change everyone involved, even when trust is broken, maybe especially then.

Whether a woman puts her faith in people, a process, or a plan, doubt will be a close kin to all. There will be ebbs and flows, highs and lows, glimpses of understanding and long slow stretches of darkness, where we mentally take ourselves by the hand and walk ourselves back to what we know to be trustworthy and true. By and by, we'll get there. To be sure, we'll recognize how both doubt and trust played their roles in helping us arrive safely. "Test everything. Hold on to the good."

Takeaway Action Thought: When in doubt, stop, pause, consider. If something is right, it can stand the wait.

Weight-Bearing Exercises

There's that old saying, "When in doubt, don't," and this catchall phrase makes perfect sense most of the time. But there's at least one area of exception to this old adage, and that area is your physical health. Whenever you have a doubt, never take the don't route. Rather, do something to get the information you need. Do call your physician, check with your pharmacist, and locate answers to your questions. Whether you're in need of an immediate reply or are looking ahead, there are answers to be found and help available. You need to know where to go and whom to trust.

Information is only as good as its source. As there are literally thousands of Internet sources available for medical information, consumers need to be leery of what they are reading and believing. A significant amount of purported medical advice is merely unsubstantiated personal opinion, and flagrant misinformation abounds. Ask yourself if the site you're researching on might have hidden agendas. Does the site's advertising parent company also sponsor the topic you are reading about? Or is the medical advice in reality an advertisement hidden in the guise of a scientific article?

≥ **Private-sector sites you can trust.** There are many good sources of accurate information for medical consumers on the Internet. Check out these sites for health-related topics applicable to women and men:

WebMD .com, HealthCentral.com, and WrongDiagnosis. com. Try HealthyWomen.org for a physician-approved site that covers a broad range of women's health issues.

❧ **Governmental websites are useful.** The National Institutes of Health site at health.nih.gov is a good general-information site with links to specific women's health issues, as well as many other useful resources.

- Peruse the hrsa.gov, the U.S. Department of Health and Human Services website, to locate links to available health care regardless of your ability to pay.

- The Centers for Disease Control and Prevention website at cdc.gov is an excellent resource for health and safety issues. This is the place to look for information on food-borne illness and any current outbreaks of this type.

- For a listing of state health agencies, go to the Food and Drug Administration's website at fda.gov/oca/ sthealth .htm.

- Local health information should be obtained through your county health department.

Teach me knowledge and good judgment.
Psalm 119:66

15

❧ FAILURE ❧
Finding Success One
Single Step at a Time

Wisdom is found along a path that is strewn
with our own sets of fears and insecurities to be
faced. We must do the thing we think we cannot
do. It's in the doing that the strength comes.
Paula Rinehart in *Strong Women, Soft Hearts*

Failure and success are two sides of the same coin (or life).
When a woman takes an accounting of her life thus far, the sum
total often is in arrears, marred by debt and default. Mistakes
and poor choices cancel out any credit-worthy contributions.
Seldom does an individual view her own worth in accurate
measure. Instead, women tend to underscore every minor or
major setback as the final, irreversible proof of a life doomed
to incalculable ruination.

The fact is, every life has its share of slippage, and in
some seasons the downfall is more costly than in others. And
yet, underlying every experience, every hardship we endure,
whether brought on by our own hand or that of another, there
is value. If we look long and hard enough, we'll discover lasting, incorruptible benefit to us and to everyone with whom we

come in contact. Hidden within every failed attempt is a greater, more resilient character being forged, and within the melding furnace of such adversity, women emerge with something priceless to pass on to others. There is a golden treasure store of hard-earned experience that comes only through pressing past inner fears and failures and insecurities.

Only if . . . we have the courage to face down those inner hesitations and that insidious hanger-on of fearful pausing that serves solely to paralyze any potential growth and progress. Only if . . . we are willing to look squarely at our decisions and take responsibility for where we are at present. Only if . . . we choose to learn from our miscalculations, our misapprehensions, our misjudgments and make purposeful corrections for the future. Only then . . . will our failures make the conversion into true successes.

As counselor Paula Rinehart kindly reminds women who struggle with overcoming the fear of repeating painful failures and past mistakes, "As long as we remain alive on the planet, faith will include fear. That we are afraid is not a mark of being insufficient to the task or made of inferior stuff. Risk is always part of the package." Rinehart then tells of another author who challenged women to quit being immobilized by their fears and failures. Rather, she instructs, move forward into whatever next step is appropriate, and "do it afraid."

Takeaway Action Thought: Count on it, if something's worthwhile, worth going after, it will entail some element of risk.

Weight-Bearing Exercises

One of Oswald Chambers's famed quotations reads, "Trust God and do the next thing." For many women, doing the next thing is something they're eager to attempt but aren't quite sure how to make the leap between setting a goal and reaching it. They've tried too many times in the past and failed ... miserably. Their confidence is flagging, and they're not even sure why they aren't being successful. Is it something lacking within them? Possibly, they only require a guided set of basic instructions to jumpstart their plan. If you find yourself ready and willing to make a change, read on.

    ❧ **When setting a goal or objective, be specific as to what you are trying to accomplish or achieve.** Focused objectives are more easily attained and more measurable. For example, if you are choosing to lose weight, set a specific number of pounds to lose, rather just taking off several pounds.

    ❧ **Make sure your goal or objective is realistic and obtainable.** If you set a goal that is too far out of your reach, it is more likely that you will not commit to completing it. If your goal is large, break it down into sections that can be achieved reasonably. As you complete each component, every small success will encourage you to conquer the next section.

    ❧ **Set a time frame to complete your goal.** Give yourself a reasonable amount of time to reach your goal. If you do not have an established deadline, you will not have a sense of urgency or the stick-to-itiveness to complete your objective. Remember that over time, your personal investment to succeed will build, as does the momentum to overcome any temporary snags or setbacks.

    ❧ **Once you have set your objective, ask yourself why you are doing it at this particular time.** Realize that outside time commitments and time constraints can interfere with even the best-laid plans. Prioritize your current obligations, and be willing to adjust your schedule accordingly. Factor in enough time in your day for things you absolutely must accomplish.

I cry out to God Most High, to God, who fulfills his purpose for me.
Psalm 57:2

❧ Part 2 ❧

SITUATIONAL LIFE CHALLENGES

16

◈ WORKPLACE ◈
How Our Talents Benefit Others Personally and Professionally

> Sometimes we need guidance over
> tough terrain, and other times all we
> really need is some company.
> Vinita Hampton Wright in *The Soul Tells a Story*

To be at one's creative best is to use gifts, talents, and innate abilities to form something, to effect a change in another person or to offer a yet undiscovered alternative to an existing idea, problem, or dilemma. Expressing one's creative bent by way of the arts (prose, music, theater) is limiting at best. Often the most telling indicators of a person's creative abilities emerge unaware to its artist. I vividly recall my electrician father poring over schematics he nightly spread across our pool table as he figured out ways to best convert or update existing electrical systems in a local plant. Even as a teenager, it wowed me to see him so lost in this work (and having the responsibility of more than two hundred workers under him impressed me even further). This memory remains one of the finest examples of creativity I can think of today. Few people would regard such labor as creative; still, by definition, my father exhibited all the traits essential to the creative process: he continually utilized imagination, visualization, problem solving, and finally execution. His work required smarts, but there was also something more enigmatic at play . . . some intangible inner gifting that allowed him to succeed where many others could not.

Herein lies the counterpart so necessary for individuals to work together well and for each to reach her or his creative potential. Few people realize how much we rely upon others to help us identify, hone, and develop our skills. How does this play out in everyday life? In a word: community. As Vinita Hampton Wright explains, "most of us need the security of at least one person who is willing to walk a step or two ahead and help us on our journey." Whether you call it mentoring, teaching, or directing, everyone benefits from the experiences of someone else who's already been where we want to end up. Wright encourages all people, no matter what her or his stage of life, to search out a person or two who might come alongside and offer timely advice and effective counsel.

According to Wright, a good mentor is someone you are comfortable with, a person who is not a major authority figure, one who truly values you and your work, is not threatened by your success, and is already a few steps ahead of you. Mutual listening and observing are also essential to this process of discovery and development.

At its best, the development of a person's gifts and their subsequent expression will result in putting people and society back together, whether this takes place on a purely aesthetic level, as in the viewing of visual art (which offers a hopeful perspective) or as a result of someone's handiwork repairing an automobile (the nuts and bolts necessary to life). Every day, every person is somehow affecting her specific sphere of influence by her attentiveness to the fullest use of her gifts or by her neglect of them. As part of community, each of us has something of value to offer, and all suffer when even a few fail to draw upon their strengths for the sake of the whole.

Takeaway Action Thought: Our individual best effort doesn't mean a whole lot if we fail to see our larger responsibility as contributing members to the community.

Weight-Bearing Exercises

While the external characteristics of our workplace do serve to define our lives in significant ways, what weighs even heavier is how we interact and view those with whom we must spend our hours and days. If we're fortunate, we work alongside individuals we respect and admire. If we're especially well-placed, we labor under the authority of individuals we respect, admire, and want to emulate in character, skill, and ability. Often, though, while our job descriptions fit the bill for our talents, workplace annoyances and misunderstandings encroach upon our emotional and mental well-being. But in all honesty, how often do we try to see a situation from the co-worker's perspective? Always? Never?

> ❧ **Never presume.** The individual who presumes to fully understand another's choices, actions, or directives before bearing that person's same responsibility generally realizes after the fact (and to her detriment) that she was wrong to assume.

> ❧ **Always give the benefit of the doubt.** Until shown otherwise, offer every person the same measure of grace you would like to receive after making a mistake.

❧ **Never discuss a private conversation publicly.** Respect every conversation as a confidence unless specifically told otherwise by the person with whom you are communicating.

❧ **Always be the first to defend another's actions.** There are always two sides, two perspectives from which every situation is perceived; get the facts equally from all the individuals involved.

❧ **Never view correction as a negative.** We don't have to agree with an individual, but we do need to listen, consider, and reach a compromise.

❧ **Always strive to be the learner in every situation.** Remember that everyone we meet has something to teach us, whether by a good example or a poor one.

It is God who arms me with strength and makes my way perfect.
Psalm 18:32

17

---

๑ CARE GIVING ๑
Proactive Planning
Takes Care of You Both

Accepting the help of others is one
of the best and most difficult ways of
fostering loving relationships.
Gary Chapman in *Love as a Way of Life*

Several years ago, forty-nine-year-old Renee had answered the call to move in with and care for her ailing and then increasingly frail eighty-year-old mother. This arrangement lasted about nine months. No sooner had Renee agreed to sell her home and join households to care for her mother than her mom changed her mind. Renee's mother decided she didn't want anyone living with her, even though she needed the assistance. After much unproductive discussion, Renee acquiesced to her mom's request and moved out of her mother's home before eventually purchasing another house for herself.

Life went on fairly smoothly during the following months, with Renee transporting her mom to appointments, doing her shopping, and making certain her mother's home was well-maintained, but Renee could see her mom couldn't live safely alone for much longer. Once again, the stress of caring for her elderly mom was affecting Renee's life.

Then Renee unexpectedly lost her job. Suddenly, her mother decided the perfect solution was for Renee to move back in with her again. Things would be different this time, her mom promised. I've changed, she told Renee. Renee wasn't so sure; then again, with the housing and job market so shaky, this might be their best option.

Weighing the pros and cons carefully, Renee decided to take pen to paper and began listing the areas that were problematic for her mom. While making such a list was semi-depressing, Renee knew it was necessary in order for her to care effectively for her mom and sustain and strengthen their sometimes tenuous relationship. Renee realized the first time around she had made certain assumptions that had ended disastrously. Not this time, she determined; both Mom and I will know going into this situation exactly what we want and expect of each other. As Renee composed her list, she recognized there were primarily three aspects of care giving, and she gave careful thought to each one based on her earlier experience.

Emotional Considerations

- ཀ Realize the parent you once knew and loved might be gone forever, and be willing to grieve the loss of that relationship even while a parent is still alive.

- ཀ Be prepared to take control of important decision making regarding all aspects of care, even when you are met with some resistance by the person in need.

- ཀ Make peace with the fact that not all extended family members will step up to assist in the way you might want and expect.

74

Spiritual Considerations

~ Before you enter into a caregiving situation, enlist the support of friends and family who will commit to pray for you and those under your care.

~ Learn how to share your faith and life perspectives without receiving the appropriate responses from the person for whom you are caring.

~ Be ready to journey along with your parents as they face their mortality, and be prepared to listen and respond to their concerns.

Physical Considerations

~ Take good care of yourself as the primary cargiver by eating right, getting enough sleep, and exercising daily.

~ Make use of professional caregiving agencies that can offer practical assistance with hygiene, dressing, and meal support.

~ Understand your personal limits before you reach them by scheduling time regularly to recharge yourself mentally and physically.

Takeaway Action Thought: For cargiving to work, it must work both ways: you give care to others, and you take care of yourself.

Weight-Bearing Exercises

One of the best practical steps to take before agreeing to become the primary cargiver to a loved one is to realize the unexpected is likely to occur. Even with the best-laid plans, life throws us curves. Sometimes a good night's sleep or a long walk will help us deal with problems. Other issues will require immediate, determined intervention and may take days or weeks to resolve. With either scenario, a good attitude and a healthy perspective, as well as the support of others, can make a world of difference. It's all about choices, those we make for ourselves and for those we care about.

Cautions on Care Giving

꙳ Providing care for a sick individual almost always requires more time and resources than most people realize.

꙳ Realize that the level of care can quickly change from minor to constant care.

꙳ Caregivers need to ask themselves if they are mentally tough enough to help with bathing, bathroom, medications, and possibly dressing changes or tubes and IV lines.

꙳ Before the cargiver becomes overwhelmed, decide ahead of time when the need for another arrangement will be required, such as transfer to a nursing home or hospice facility.

꙳ Plan for unexpected expenses to arise from a variety of sources.

꙳ When cargivers begin feeling frustrated, anxious, or depressed, note these as warning signs that the situation must be promptly addressed and responsibilities reduced.

꙳ No one individual should assume the cargiver role without some form of backup, even for a short time.

ॐॐॐॐ
Surely God is my help; the Lord is the one who sustains me.
Psalm 54:4

18

∻ PARENTING ∽
What We Believe Shouts

> Talk is not cheap because interpretation
> is not cheap. The way we interpret life
> determines how we will respond to it.
> Paul David Tripp in *War of Words*

What we expect as normal behavior for children when they are young we come to resent as they grow older, and this orientation of our hearts as parents shows up most clearly through our words. A small child who speaks before thinking, even when he says something hurtful, is excused with a gentle reprimand and a caution to think before he talks next time around. Grace seems to come easily to parents of younger children because parents know over time and with maturity, they can expect more of their youngsters.

There is nothing wrong with this line of thinking, until the young children reach an age where parents know the kids know better . . . but choose irresponsibility, laziness, selfishness, or foolishness. Swiftly, parental patience descends into impatience, irritation, and an all-out war of words. Communication breaks down or fails. Words become weapons. Both parents and their kids quickly draw lines of combat, and neither side emerges unscathed.

The truth is, parents expect something out of parenting that doesn't happen. Kids don't suddenly make the transformation from delightful, fun-loving, non-offensive children into delightful, mature, non-offensive young adults. There is a spectrum of parenting and parental responsibility. Our misconception, then, is that as parents, we believe we can pass over this great divide with minimal conflict and sacrifice to our own parental comfort. Be honest, we do.

As kids reach their teen years, a sudden shift takes place in a parent's heart and mind . . . we say in our hearts, our job is just about over, and our kids' behavior better reflect this faulty but desperately coveted desire. Sure, we want our children to evidence ever-growing steps toward maturity, and they should do so, but when they don't keep in step, how do we react? Do we respond in anger when they interrupt our desire for a peaceful evening? Are we visibly upset that they require our time when we're already exhausted? Can they see our irritation spill over when they didn't listen (again) and we have to implement the needed corrective discipline?

This raging conflict between our expectations and the reality of parenting children through to adulthood is where many moms and dads give up before the job is done. Clearly, one of the most obvious methods parents use to employ their dissatisfaction and give their termination notice is through their words. What lies in the heart truly does come out of the mouth, often gushing forth during moments of physical and emotional exhaustion. It's wearying to contemplate, let alone discuss. But discuss we must, first in our hearts and minds, then through our words and deeds.

Paul Tripp explains this important link between heart and mouth: "Whatever controls our hearts will control our words. In fact, you could argue that if a certain desire controls my heart, there are only two ways I can respond to you. If you help me get what I want, I will enjoy and appreciate you. But if you stand in my way, I will experience (and probably express) anger when you are around."

The question is, will parents willingly re-enter the fray of parenting, uncomfortable though it may be, or will their words communicate their desire to abdicate their parental responsibility too soon? When kids get in the way, and especially then, they will recognize the difference between a parent's cheaply offered lip service and the costly, sacrificially offered alternative. As the writer of Proverbs states, "Words kill, words give life; they're either poison or fruit—you choose" (Proverbs 18:21, MSG).

Takeaway Action Thought: The old adage, "Actions speak louder than words," could use a revision," "Actions speak as loudly as words." Our words matter.

Weight-Bearing Exercises

Every woman wants her kids to grow up strong, healthy, and able to communicate effectively with the world at large. Beginning on the inside and working out means helping youngsters take responsibility for their actions as well as their words. From the time they are small, moms commit themselves to caring for their children body and soul and preparing them for life's challenges. How can moms help raise kids who understand the implications of their words and their choices? Read on.

My Words Count

➷ Responsibility always begins with self. As the parent, be willing to do a mental inventory of how often (and how loudly) you communicate instructions, directions, and verbal warnings.

➷ Ask yourself how it would feel to be on the receiving end of your talk (factor in your tone of voice as well as your physical demeanor that frequently speaks volumes more than your words).

➷ Be honest enough to admit that no one speaks lovingly 100% of the time and learn to play back your conversations. If necessary, hit the rewind as many times as needed to get it right.

Your Words Count

➷ When kids speak with disrespect or lack of courtesy, put a halt to it immediately. Similar to the fireman's drill of stop, drop, and roll, implement a stop, silence, and think rule.

➷ In those moments when tempers flare, preempt a full-blown fight with a pre-assigned hand signal that everyone in the family clearly understands. Call a timeout before words get flung that can't be taken back.

➷ Learn to ask your kids this key question, "How would you feel if I said the words you just spoke to me, back to you?" Then discuss how they could have communicated the same message differently. Practice can make perfect (almost).

How sweet are your words to my taste,
sweeter than honey to my mouth!
Psalm 119:103

19

ᕲ FINANCIAL SETBACKS ᕘ
How Material Wealth Insulates Us from What Matters Most

> We are not just physical stuff; we are
> spiritual beings. And our deepest hunger
> is spiritual. We hunger for meaning. We
> hunger for love. We hunger for redemption.
> John Ortberg in *When the Game Is
> Over It All Goes Back in the Box*

Philosophers and theologians alike have long asserted and clung to the nonsensical notion that it is somehow beneath people of true character to acquire or require any form of material wealth. In their attempt to warn their followers of succumbing to insatiable greediness, those who propose that money and what it provides human beings are wholly unnecessary couldn't be farther from the mark. True enough, the lure of wealth in any form can slowly rob an individual of her life's genuine and ever-lasting treasures. And yet, in this real world inhabited by real people, there is a real need for money. Like it or not, financial wealth is the currency we live by, and there's no disputing it. The distinctive point is not whether we need money or not; we all do. The argument, then, is that individuals shouldn't spend their entire life's energy fighting to get an increasingly larger share to covetously hoard. Everyone will admit there is more to life than the material substances we can see, taste, and touch. Still, there can be no denying that money is a great insulator. It offers us food, shelter, clothing, and a whole lot more. It protects from us lacking the same, and a whole lot more.

This "whole lot more" supposition is where the crux of the caution lies. Money can feed our bodies, but it does nothing for the soul, and we might well observe that the current state of our economy is pressing hard this very point. As hardworking men and women stand to lose much of their earnings, we are all discovering how much value we've placed on this single-faceted entity. Maybe it's not possible to see it clearly because we live in the most prosperous nation on earth. Certainly, the loss of savings hurts, but can it heal? Can we allow our diminishing financial investments to nudge us toward greater ones, ones that outlive us?

We might ask ourselves if we are so used to being comfortable financially that as we lose this insulating buffer, we are at a loss to know how to function well or function at all. This insidious reaction should warn and serve to alert us. The financial setback in reality might set us back enough that we have no other choice but to make some changes, some soul-searching ones. Once we recover, and we will, what then? Will we revert to this earlier insular mindset?

Whether it's a little or a lot, money in itself is never fully satisfying. We can wear ourselves thin attempting to make more, invest more, and make it multiply faster. But more is never enough when all you're aiming at is being satiated with money for money's sake. John Ortberg observes with irony, "That's the world in which we live: we sell what nobody needs. But the problem of the human heart is: we need what nobody sells."

Takeaway Action Thought: Reduce your expenses by reducing your appetites throughout every area of life; learn to equate reduction with freedom.

Weight-Bearing Exercises

When hard times hit, people try hard to save money wherever and whenever they can. They trim budgets, go out less, and make longer use of the material goods they already own. In similar fashion, when economic times get leaner, taking care of one's physical health is reduced on the priority list. Still, there are some easy and simple ways to maintain excellent health. Look over the suggestions below for some of the cheapest ways to stay healthy.

- **Bonuses:** Staying fit and healthy does not have to be expensive or complicated. The easiest, most natural way to get good exercise is to walk at least several times a week. You burn the same amount of calories walking a mile as you do running. Walking also serves as a double-duty exercise, as it offers both aerobic and weight-bearing exercise benefits. Not only is walking good for your heart and waistline; it is good for bone health as well.

- **Home savings:** No one needs a pricy gym membership when you can work out at home. When the weather is moderate, get outside daily for that multibeneficial walk. If the weather is bad, go to the local mall and walk indoors. Another option is to check out various types of exercise videos from your local library to offer some variety. No matter what type of exercise you choose, statistics show that you will be more likely to stay with the program if you establish a regular schedule and stick to it. Another bonus to working out at home is that it eliminates extra barriers such as inclement weather and constraints of travel time.

❧ **Market smarts:** When it comes to healthy eating, it is quite simple: eat a balanced diet. Focus on the fresh and unprocessed. Typically, fruits and vegetables are good sources of nutrition. Diet food tends to be more expensive and generally is no better for you than standard fare. As a rule, when you avoid processed food (think: those foods that come out of a box), you will be eating a healthy diet. Forgo bottled water or soda. Opt for lots of plain tap water instead; your body needs it, and it is free.

❧❧❧❧

Whom have I in heaven but you? And earth
has nothing I desire besides you.
Psalm 73:25

20

❧ RELOCATION ❧
Moving for the Right Reasons

> Life always plays in a forward direction;
> it never goes backward. Once a move
> is made, there is no going back.
> John Ortberg in *When the Game Is*
> *Over It All Goes Back in the Box*

How we move. Have you ever watched how we women move? How often, how fast, and sometimes how far? It's an amazing cultural phenomenon. The more transient our society becomes, the more urgently we opt for address changes, the more it tells about us and how less likely it is that we will stay put long enough to weather the important seasons of life with one another, that is. What used to be a given, that assumption of sticking together and staying put come what may, is no longer taken for granted and has bled into our worldview.

People used to expect to grow up, grow close, and grow old together. But now it's interesting to listen to women with young adult children converse. They don't even foresee or dare to hope their kids will land somewhere near the town where they were raised. While moving isn't bad, it can be disruptive: to the kids and their friends, to the grandparents and other extended relatives, to the parents and to one's self. It all depends.

Sometimes moving is a good thing, when it's chosen for the right reason, at the appropriate time, and when given careful, thoughtful consideration. Moving to a new home or apartment, in town or out in the country, to a different city or across the state, picking up and transplanting can be the next best step in a person's life journey. The real dilemma, then, is learning to weigh one's choices, one's motives for packing up and setting off, because no matter how good another locale appears, everyone knows the landing is the same. The aesthetics might be different, more palatable for a while, but once the newness wears off and routine settles in, what then? Can we live with our choice, or will we start contemplating our next best point of future relocation?

We can't always see what's best for us and those we love. So, before we uproot, it's good to gather the people who love us most and know us best for some community brainstorming. We give and take best when we're ready and willing to receive hard counsel that might say, "Stop," "Wait," or "Don't." It's often far less painful this way too.

Wherever we decide we want to hang our hats, location is important. Where we choose to live, or where we decide to move, matters, to us and to everyone whose lives we will touch along the way. Moving and staying can be painful and not mutually exclusive, but as long as our lives are moving forward (inside our head and hearts), that's what counts.

Takeaway Action Thought: When we're careful to move for the right reasons and in the right way, the relocation won't hurt.

Weight-Bearing Exercises

Given our generation's propensity for change, it is a given that we'll either move or assist someone else making a move. So, what are some practical considerations to keep in mind as we begin making plans to transport both the large and the small to another location? Read below . . . and be careful to move with care. You're of no real help to another if you push too hard, too fast, and get injured. Balance is key. Make it your relocation motto today.

How We Move

༠ Try not to lift with the back bent. Use the legs, and keep the weight close to your body to reduce strain. Avoid twisting while lifting; use your feet to turn your body.

༠ A woman should lift no more than one third of her body weight.

༠ If you begin to develop severe back pain or pain that radiates down one of your legs, stop immediately. Also, if you are not used to repetitive or heavy lifting, expect to be sore for the next several days.

༠ For day-after pain relief, try an over-the-counter anti-inflammatory if you do not have bleeding problems or sensitivity to this type of medication. Acetaminophen can also be helpful. Applying warm, moist heat can be soothing and relaxing.

I will instruct you and teach you in the way you should
go; I will counsel you and watch over you.
Psalm 32:8

87

21

⮞ DIVORCE & WIDOWHOOD ⮜
When Friends Secure
the Gap

> That is what our friendship groups
> are. They are our safety nets. Because
> sometimes you fall so hard that you need
> more than one person to catch you.
> Sarah Zacharias Davis in *The Friends We Keep*

When women get married, we don't expect to get divorced. When women marry, we don't expect to live a portion of our life alone. Such dread developments don't appear on many women's mental radars, especially at the beginning of our relationships. Over time, when a marriage unravels or a spouse dies, women have no option but to face the unexpected. The "what was" of our lives isn't true any longer, and the roles we slowly eased into with a partner are suddenly and swiftly gone. The relational rhythms women grew accustomed to over perhaps many years abruptly cease to exist. The unexpected and unanticipated is our newly unfamiliar companion.

These types of loss are significantly life-altering and can shatter even the most resilient of women. So, where does a woman turn when her life and the love of it bottoms out? The smartest and safest place a woman goes is to her friends, immediately, without hesitation, and with no holding back. With other females is where this woman, any woman, will find her safety net of protection, provision, and quite possibly some pressure. Good friends will lovingly pressure her to keep going, to not give up, or to resist embracing a soloist mentality, because isolation is every woman's worst enemy.

Women and our friendships: Our solidarity is confounding, given that we often agree and disagree in equal measure, yet our loyalty pronounces a unity that can't be disputed. Good friends won't let each other fall too far. We have each other's backs. We feel each other's pain. Friends sometimes feel like a pain, true enough. And still, when the losses tally up, women rally to one another's sides, and we secure the gap with a commitment so tenacious it can be startling to onlookers as well as to us. Women reach out and secure one another. We reach under and lift up. We reach around and hold tight. Surrounded by such a safety net and secured by unconditional love, it's no wonder that women fare better than our male counterparts in the wake of similarly devastating circumstances. There is indeed safety in numbers.

Sarah Zacharias Davis observes how even after traumatic loss, the language of friendships can offer something precious, not to replace the loss, mind you, but to circumvent some measure of the hurt. "Friendship love speaks of listening, honesty, forgiveness, giving the benefit of the doubt, and sacrifice. It is standing and declaring publicly, '*This is my friend.*'" Real friends make a woman feel safe, in season and out.

Takeaway Action Thought: Friends are those we choose to walk with us throughout all of life's highs and lows, so invest with common sense and care.

Weight-Bearing Exercises

Upon the heels of any major life change or loss, it is possible for women to get edgy, fearful, all-around tentative; what used to work doesn't anymore, and we find ourselves second-guessing ourselves, our safety, our independence. Add aging to the mix, and some suddenly-single women grow terrified of living alone. Read on to learn important considerations and questions to ask when deciding whether it's safe or not. Remember, every woman's most reliable safety nets are common sense, friends, and family.

> ๙ **Common sense—day to day.** If you choose to remain in your own home and are at a high risk for falling; it is always recommended that you obtain a medical-alert system. If a fall occurs, you the hit the button, and help will arrive. Resist the "it will never happen to me" refrain, and be proactively smart and safe. Also, understand that getting proper nutrition becomes increasingly difficult as women age. Make the most of your community's services that offer meals for seniors that are delivered daily for a reasonable price.

> ๙ **Friends and family—company and care.** If you continue living alone, be realistic about how much support family and friends can reasonably provide. If someone needs to check on you daily or throughout the day, then you are not truly independent, even if you still live by yourself. Family members may agree to check in and oversee care, but you need to care enough about their welfare to see the additional stress it creates in their lives. Communicate honestly, and make every effort to remain flexible and open to discussing alternatives that work best for everyone involved.

🔊 **Ask yourself—and be honest.** Am I really better off living alone? Am I safe? Am I able to get proper nutrition? If you answer no to any of these questions, think twice (and yet again) about living on your own. Most people try to hold on to their independence too long. Not surprisingly, when people make the transition from home to assisted living, they achieve an overall higher quality of life because their stress level is dramatically decreased. Just knowing someone is there close by to help makes all the difference.

A father to the fatherless, a defender of widows, is God
in his holy dwelling. God sets the lonely in families.
Psalm 68:5–6

22

ᠵ RETIREMENT ᠵ
Kindness Is
Age-Resistant

> Life is committed relationships of self-giving
> love with those whom you would normally not
> hang out with: those whom you don't always
> like; those who don't share your zip code.
> Leonard Sweet in *So Beautiful*

For too long, retirement has been viewed as "my time," but statistics show that those retirees who retire from (that is, stop) using those skills and abilities they honed and developed over the years in the work field suffer from a myriad of self-imposed ills.

So it's official now: proffering acts or words of kindness is healthful. For starters, there's the biblical injunction that it is more blessed to give than receive, and let's not forget that it's inhumane and soul-searing to observe another person struggling without offering some form of aid or relief. Then there's the internal physiological reward of having done a good deed that makes a person want to give a repeat performance. This feel-good emotion has been dubbed a "helper's high" by Allan Luks, author of *The Healing Power of Doing Good.* This sudden release of endorphins is comparable to a runner's high and is similarly characterized by experiencing an initial rush of euphoria followed by an inner calm that enhances and stabilizes emotional well-being long after the deed is done. According to the Random Acts of Kindness Foundation, multiple, additional physiological factors occur after a person performs a kind act. It matters not whether you're male or female (this is an equal-opportunity benefit) or if you even know the person you are helping (most individuals don't). However, increased frequency of volunteerism brings about higher and longer-lasting health benefits, so adopting an altruistic lifestyle, which is consistently represented by the extending of oneself on behalf of another, is a no-lose venture.

Men and women alike can expect to experience more emotional resilience while reducing negativity and hostility. They may likewise discover that their good deeds will be far-reaching enough to lower their incidences of headaches, backaches, depression, colds and flu, and arthritic problems. Luks believes that there is a correlation between these benefits and a person's outlook on life in general. If one believes she is making a difference, her internal framework responds toward that inclination. Luks's studies have shown that do-gooders enjoy a stronger immune system. There is a decrease in the intensity or awareness of physical pain, positive emotions are activated while negative ones diminish, and bodily stress is relieved. Perhaps one of the strongest statements for appropriating random acts of kindness into one's everyday existence is that "the health benefits and sense of well-being return for hours or even days whenever the act is remembered." In other words, the good stuff trails in your wake and becomes the impetus for even more genuine acts of kindness.

Takeaway Action Thought: Everyone gains when you kindheartedly opt back into active service and continue to use your abilities to benefit others.

Weight-Bearing Exercises

How would a life change, my life and yours, if we all adopted the "always on call" outlook? Every time we step out the door, log online, answer the phone, or talk with a family member, we can aim to see and serve. We won't be content with observing the surface-y stuff but will see into the deepest needs of the person in front of us and then begin to meet those needs. It means, of course, coming out of retirement for good. No matter how young or old we are, we never rest from our obligations to serve those around us. As long as we have breath, we have a responsibility to use the gifts we've been given to better someone else's life. If you've given into the "my time" retirement mentality, read on for some everyday ways to step out of retirement and back into life.

- **Keep your eyes open to the needs and dispositions of others.** Make it a discipline to ask yourself how you might lighten the burdens of the person in front of you in such a way that she or he will feel its positive effect immediately.

- **Listen to what someone is telling you, beyond the scope of what she or he verbalizes.** Develop a more keen sensitivity as you engage others in conversation. Keep asking yourself, what is the emotion behind the catchphrases? What is the real need of this person's heart today?

- **Be willing to extend yourself, even if it means setting aside your agenda.** Retirees are notorious for getting into a scheduling rut and not budging . . . for anything, even when the television guide is what is governing their schedule.

- **Remember and reflect on those moments when someone extended kindness in your direction.** If you get stuck trying to figure out practical ways to make a difference, go no further than your own experience as being on the receiving end of another's goodwill. Remember and repeat. And repeat some more.

ॐ **Focus on living with an other-ness lifestyle every day.** Determine to come out and stay out of retirement. Seek out those opportunities for regular service using your particular abilities to benefit others in same measure as you did when employed. The benefits will be far richer.

I was young and now I am old, yet I have never seen the righteous forsaken or their children begging bread. They are always generous and lend freely.
Psalm 37:25, 26

23

---

৯ CAREER CHOICES ৶
How People Factor into a
Satisfactory Workplace

You cannot self-generate the necessary "heat"
of affirmation, encouragement, and support
that are gained from true friendship.
David H. McKinley in *The Search for Satisfaction*

If you keep tabs on the daily Internet news leads, it's clear the writers of these career primers believe that experiencing success, satisfaction, or even workplace satiation boils down to gaining three objectives: money, power, and prestige. Almost every career advancement tip is carefully coiffed, meticulously scripted, and laced with predatory implications: it's me against you, and, if given the choice, I won't allow you a foothold. The truth is, these writers aren't even close to assessing correctly what men and women cite as the most satisfying aspect of their career.

Can you guess? Hands down, it's how successful individuals measure their interaction with others and how great an effect they believe they make day in and day out. It doesn't matter if a person spends the bulk of his time in a business, medical, educational, service, or media workplace. The conclusion is the same: how richly we relate to others makes all the difference. Not only does enjoying vibrant relationships with one's colleague's determine how individuals quantify their level of happiness, but it also affects how productive they are. McKinley writes, "Doing the job alone—is a primary cause for lack of productivity in our lives." So instead of vying for that next promotion in too typical lone-ranger fashion, employers and employees would be better served to focus their energies on upping their people-service quotient as they work with and for those around them.

On the Job: What's Most Satisfying?

- ❧ Developing relationships with parents and students. (academic advisor)

- ❧ Helping people get through a difficult time in life. (physician)

- ❧ Affecting lives for the good. (salon owner)

- ❧ Supporting people as they change. (family counselor)

- ❧ Presenting a package, then watching the recipient unwrap the gift. (college art professor)

- ❧ Knowing something made a difference. (writer)

- ❧ Finding the right solution to a client's problem. (national account executive)

- ❧ Instructing children and cheering their progress. (media secretary)

- ❧ Seeing the visual satisfaction of my customers. (gardener/landscaper)

- ❧ Creating or inventing product that brings value to my company and its people. (chief architect)

On the Job: What's Most Difficult?

ॐ Dealing with people in crises who have no support system. (critical care registered nurse)

ॐ Trying to help people who will not help themselves or make no effort to take responsibility for their own problems. (surgeon)

ॐ Absent students and discipline problems. (secondary teacher)

ॐ Experiencing isolation from others by working from home. (real estate developer)

ॐ Having to say no to 2500 inquiries or proposals a year. (acquisitions manager)

ॐ Convincing the needy or elderly that they require assistance. (owner of home health care business)

ॐ Getting others to catch the vision and invest in it. (publisher)

Do you notice the common thread? Work gratification is all about developing and maintaining significant relationships with others and using one's gifts and talents along the way. There's no mention of money here, not a single reference to stepping up the ladder of success. When we operate under the principle of partnering with people for the benefit of all, everyone wins. And when people feel like winners, even mediocre work relationships transform into rich resources of friendship. McKinley notes, "Life is full of treacherous pathways. The potential for a fall is great. We need friends who can help us and provide strength in times of weakness, so don't travel alone." Even if those career advancement experts were even a little bit right, they were mostly wrong. Aren't you glad?

Takeaway Action Thought: Learn to measure success beyond that of solely achieving tangible work goals. Broaden the definition to include the ultimately more satisfying people factor.

Weight-Bearing Exercises

Whether you are satisfied with your current workplace environment or have one foot (mentally or physically) out the door; periodically assessing the physical and emotional demands your career places on you each day makes good sense. Before you contemplate a change in your vocation or pursue a new direction, walk through the following checklist of workplace health considerations.

- ⁊ If your job is sedentary, make sure you get up at least once every hour to stretch and move around to get circulation going and re-energize you mentally.

- ⁊ If your job involves lots of activity, be sure to wear clothing and shoes that allow for flexibility and don't obstruct movement or balance.

- ⁊ Consider your current physical health and age before you change careers. Assess yourself accurately as to whether or not you are fit enough for the job you desire.

- ⁊ Ask yourself if there are stresses in your workplace that detract from your overall health picture, and work to change or eliminate these risks.

- ⁊ Think about the emotional temperature of your workplace and how it either cools you off or sets you on fire. Is conflict resolution encouraged or discouraged, and is there a plan in place? Work to develop one if needed.

But I am trusting in you, O Lord, saying, "You are my God!" My times are in your hands.
Psalm 31:14–15

24

⁊ PHYSICAL ILLNESS ⁊
How Your Social Environment Can Make You Sick

> For all of us, there are inevitable moments
> when, even surrounded by loving family
> and friends, we feel invisible or go through
> something alone. A surgery, a divorce, a death,
> a failure. Those sleepless nights, those closet
> moments, those tears we shed in private.
> Carolyn Custis James in *Lost Women of the Bible*

Just how important is environment to a woman's health? We're not talking here about buildings with lead paint and moldy closets and corners. Instead, environment is the people we work with and for each day, the family we come home to every evening, and the friends we willingly associate with whenever we can. This is our environment, for better or worse.

And why does it matter so much? Environment is important for one primary reason. Every environment a woman finds herself in or remains in is either for or against her. There's rarely a middle ground, and depending upon whether or not her surroundings are favorable to her (toward her), everything changes, for better or worse.

Perhaps a better question, then, is this: How long does it take for a woman to realize her environment might be making her physically sick and heartsick alike? For some, it can mean a lifetime of slowly sinking or feeling diminished at work, in the home, or at the hands of some person she's given far too much control over her. For others, the wake-up comes in short order, and this woman starts making plans. As soon as she does, she begins seeing changes occur, for the better.

Women who are not in the right place or among the right people place themselves at risk, all kinds of risks, physical and emotional. A long-term, debilitating effect occurs when women remain in an environment that works against us, for the worse.

So, how does a woman know when her environment has turned hostile toward her? She asks herself some telling questions. How does she feel before entering said surroundings? Is she able to use her gifts, talents, or abilities in good measure while present there? Does she exit the locale confident she's left it in better condition, or worse?

When we spend our hours and days in situations and among people who devalue, disrespect, or dishonor us, it hurts physically and emotionally. When we are not being seen for who we are by those who matter the most to us, is it little wonder that emotional and physical illnesses present themselves? Larry Julian sums this up nicely: "Our environment provides the trigger that sparks the best (and the worst) in us." The question, then, is: What response does your environment trigger in you? Are you able to say definitively, it's for the better?

Takeaway Action Thought: Ask yourself if the environment you are in has been promoting your overall health and well-being or detracting from it. Let your history speak for itself.

Weight-Bearing Exercises

Women long to be known and understood for who we are, no matter what environment we are in. Among family or friends, women are relational; we thrive on building long-standing histories with one another. But beyond this strength of relational community, women also need to know what types of physical illnesses are part of our family history. In other words, a woman's relatives (and their relative health) can make a difference. See below for some of the top health-related reasons it's essential to know and understand the physical history of your immediate and extended family members. Even when we might fear the worst, knowing is best.

ॐ While risk factors for disease can be attributed to numerous factors such as age, nutrition, and environmental exposure; genetics, or family history, is likely the most compelling factor for risk of disease.

ॐ Knowing your family history can provide valuable information for your physician. Certain cancers and medical problems require routine screening per recommended guidelines that are often accelerated for certain medical problems based on family history.

ॐ To the patient, this means that those individuals with a strong family history often require earlier or more frequent screening. Family history of colon cancer is one such disease. If early screening is instituted, it may allow diagnosis and treatment of a condition when it is at an earlier, more treatable stage.

☞ Important: knowledge of family medical history can assist your physician in making a diagnosis that may not otherwise be considered. Therefore, whenever possible, it is valuable to document the medical problems of your parents and siblings and take this information to your physician.

O LORD, you have searched me and you know me.
Psalm 139:1

25

❧ RELATIONAL STRESS ❧
How Our Pain Levels Us

> Feelings, and feelings, and feelings.
> Let me try thinking instead.
> C. S. Lewis in *A Grief Observed*

If someone asked you how you were feeling, you'd answer without hesitation, right? If someone asked you what you were thinking, would you know what to say? If someone asked what you thought and felt about a given situation, what then? Would you in any way be able to offer a reply that communicates the problem with any accuracy, or would your feelings override the facts?

For it is a matter of fact that whenever we're in a tight spot with another person, backed against a wall and feeling pushed, prodded, or pressed, our feelings hit overdrive. All we can think about is how this person or the position she's placed us in make us feel. We feel and feel and feel some more. It doesn't take long for our feelings to hold sway over our thoughts or the facts of the matter.

Thinking through the issue doesn't often occur to us until we've had our say and thrown some thoughtless wrecking balls. Then we are left feeling frustrated about the initial problem and frustrated with ourselves because we do know better than to give full vent to our feelings. We don't want to be stopped when we're feeling pushed, prodded, or pressed about a topic, a person, a cause, or a dilemma. We prefer having our say. It feels so good getting our thoughts out.

At least, it feels good in the moment, but give the words some time to settle in, and these impulsive utterances feel anything but good. We wonder why we didn't keep silent or walk away and gain control of our emotions before we opened our mouth. Silence truly can be golden, a golden opportunity that is, to think long and hard. We ask ourselves, Why didn't we stop and think first? Think, think, and think some more.

Whatever your relational stress looks like, silence (initiating and maintaining it) at the right moment can make all the difference. Sometimes all everyone needs is a few minutes or hours, days even, to retreat, consider, and reflect. Pushing someone to make a decision, take a side, or reply before he's ready only makes an already uncomfortable discussion all the more emotionally volatile.

Silence is not defeat. It is not weakness, nor is it giving way. Rather, it is making way. It is taking the necessary time to be quiet enough to figure out the next step. Silence is comparable to making a battle plan, though it is not to be confused with the aggressive stance of waging war. Rather, it is to obtain a peaceful outcome. Sister Wendy Beckett observes, "There is nothing casual about silence. In its peace, it is productive. It prepares us for whatever is to come. Silence is, in itself, armor."

Silence is taking time to carefully think about the situation from the other person's position. It is thinking about what part we might have had in contributing to the issue. It is thinking about how we might make amends. It is thinking about the best way to ask for forgiveness. In this order, choose silence first, then think it through. Feelings will follow.

Takeaway Action Thought: When we are feeling pain of any sort, sometimes the biggest challenge is to decide whether it serves best to speak or be silent.

Weight-Bearing Exercises

Be honest: who hasn't had running through the back of her mind this generalized statement, "This is such a pain"? Whether it's accurate or not (about a person or a situation) is another question, for this type of internal dialogue is generally a subjective observation dependent upon a woman's mood and how she's feeling that day about life overall. Pain of all kinds fluctuates. So, does the same principle hold true when women experience physical pain? Is there a trustworthy gauge or guide? How can a woman accurately communicate her pain levels to others, to her physician in particular? Read below to better understand what a physician silently thinks in answer to a patient's description of her pain.

~ When communicating pain scales, it's important to be realistic. Exaggerated numbers do not impress physicians. In fact, doctors will be less inclined to believe patients are credible if they tend to exaggerate.

~ For reference, the definition of Level 10 pain is "pain so intense you will go unconscious shortly." This type of pain occurs in those who have suffered a severe accident with multiple broken bones or injury such as a crushed hand or leg.

~ Most people come to a physician's office with Level 6 pain or less.

∂ Clues as to how much pain someone is in come from nonverbals such pacing or rocking, difficulty thinking clearly or rationally, and difficulty speaking due to waves of pain or shortness of breath.

∂ If your pain is truly Level 7 or greater, you should be in the emergency department and not in a doctor's office.

∾∾∾∾

O God, do not keep silent; be not quiet, O God, be not still.
Psalm 83:1

26

☙ AGING ❧
Making Good Choices, Lifelong Good Habits

> You are capable of taking every situation
> in your life and representing it in a way
> that will lead to joy or to despair. The
> interpretation is in your hands.
> Richard L. Ganz in *The Secret of Self-Control*

When Kelly walked into her mom's private room, she couldn't believe the change. Counting back in her mind, she revisited the last time she'd been with her mother since her mom's fall three weeks earlier. Four days? That's it? She had to be mistaken. How could her mom have seemingly aged years in mere days? But she had.

Kelly moved closer to her mother's sleeping figure and tentatively reached out to touch her hand, so cold. Kelly carefully pulled the blanket over her mom's arms and sat down at her bedside. Not wanting to wake her, Kelly simply sat. Stunned, yes, but also grateful for the time she had to process what she was seeing. She had a hard time absorbing this sudden deterioration and wondered when it would end, if it would end?

What had happened to her once-vibrant and so-active mom? How did this fall send her into a nursing home with a grim statistic for full recovery looming over all their heads? Kelly sat pensively revisiting the past ten years or so, when her mom first got the news that she had developed lung cancer. Always a smoker, Kelly's mom had tried to quit countless times through the years, but her efforts never lasted long enough to get the smell of smoke off her clothing. Kelly didn't have room to fault her mom there . . . she was a smoker too . . . maybe not as heavy, but she still indulged the habit.

Even after her mom had part of one lung removed, she soon went right back to her cigarettes. She didn't seem to listen when her doctor told her that her bones were getting thinner either. That is, she didn't take the medicines prescribed to her, nor did she get onto the exercise program recommended. Kelly and her sisters tried talking to their mom, tried reasoning with her, but she ignored them and told her daughters she'd be fine once she got her strength back.

Well, sitting here isn't fine, not one bit fine, Kelly thought angrily. We didn't do enough, and we sure didn't insist on Mom taking better care of herself. But who am I to judge? That could be me in another twenty years . . . or not. Kelly started to work through her shock that quickly edged into fear. I don't want Mom to continue on a headlong road to total incapacitation just because she's too stubborn to give up her bad habits.

We're going to make some changes, all of us, and help each other stay on track. It's not too late to try, and that's going to be the one message Mom will have to get used to hearing until she believes it, until we all do.

"A basic truth is always at work—old habits die hard. Consider your life. You've watched your habits. You've watered them. You've nurtured and pruned them. You've helped them blossom," writes Ganz.

Takeaway Action Thought: Good habits or bad, they're never so entrenched that they can't be changed.

Weight-Bearing Exercises

Everyone knows that habits are powerful forces that serve to make or break a person's ability to live optimally through every stage of life. Whether a woman's highest aim is to successfully manage her own business, run a marathon, or serve her community, she had better become a quick study of those habits that will aid in achieving her goals by fortifying body and soul. Aging comes to everyone, but no one ages in the same way. It is up to each of us to do the best with what we've been given. To start and finish well, make a mental note to remind yourself to put the following recommendations into practice.

Habits That Give You Control

&- Walk or exercise several times weekly.

Statistic: With 1,440 minutes in every day, allotting 30 minutes to exercise is a small investment that reaps high gains.

&- Take calcium with Vitamin D supplements daily.

Statistic: Women should take 1,500 mg of calcium and 800 mg of vitamin D supplements per day to help prevent osteoporosis.

🕭 Do not smoke.

Statistic: Approximately 23 million (that's 23 percent of the female population) of American women still smoke cigarettes despite the widely known risk factors for developing cancer.

🕭 Get adequate sleep.

Statistic: Most women need between seven and eight hours per night. Sound, restful slumber can be negatively affected by certain medications, illness, hormones, stress, poor sleep habits, and depression.

🕭 Eat a well-balanced diet.

Statistic: Women need to eat breakfast every day and need to eat proportionally from all six food groups: grains, vegetables, fruits, milk, meats and beans, and oils. See www.mypyramid.gov for the new U.S.D.A. food pyramid. You can even enter in your information and get a customized food guide of how much you need from each food group.

🕭 Drink plenty of water.

Statistic: In general, women require approximately eight 8-ounce glasses of water every day, remembering that needs can vary according to fluctuations in exercise, environment, and illness or heath conditions. Try carrying around a water bottle with measurement marks on the side, so you can keep track of whether you've gotten your full 64 ounces.

The Lord gives strength to his people; the
Lord blesses his people with peace.
Psalm 29:11

27

❧ CHILDREARING ❧
When Parents Pass on the Torch of Responsibility

> Absorbing the mess is just part of
> the process of getting close.
> Philip Yancey in *Rumors of Another World*

Kids make messes. Some we can laugh about, others, not so much. Little kids with chocolate-smeared faces and sticky fingers can make us smile. Big kids with bad attitudes, failing grades, and a speeding ticket can make us weep. Messes are a part of life, and we might well ask how much of our time is spent cleaning them up, our messes and those of our kids. If we're honest, sometimes the two overlap, and maybe, just maybe . . . our parental messes cause or provoke some of those our kids get mired in—then again, maybe not.

Either way, a mess of any significant proportion has to be faced and dealt with sooner rather than later. As parents, we want to believe that we've done all we can to prepare our children for adulthood and for that next step of independence they're continually clamoring for. And yet, when we adopt that "let me fix it for you" response to our older children's actions, it gives us away. At this important juncture, we must ask ourselves hard questions. Are we enabling (excusing) or ennobling (exhorting) our offspring through our intervention? Mind-boggling, isn't it, the mess we make by not understanding the difference?

Moms enable their kids when they excuse or make excuses for their children's poor choices. Moms can ennoble their kids by doing precisely the opposite. Women who give way and make excuses for their kids' behavior find it is easier in the short run. The kids don't grouse or complain, and they walk away feeling like they got away with something. Yet, we know they didn't, and they know they didn't. There's no escaping from the repercussions of our decisions, be they little or large, and to give kids a false sense of security on this front is mindlessly shortsighted at best. At worst, the messes our kids will make with their lives if they believe they can do what they want, when they want, and with whom they want will only hurt them and others over the long stretch of adulthood.

Kids with moms who perpetually clean up after them are, or likely will be, young adults who are ill-equipped to stay in school, enter the job force, or sustain any type of lasting relationship, especially when life gets messy-hard (and it will). Their messes will continue to getter bigger and more confounding, with ever-widening circles of clutter. Eventually, no one, not even their family, will want to get close enough to even attempt to unravel the monstrosity.

When moms excuse their kids from living responsibly, it's a case of benign neglect, which in medical terms means watching a problem clinically without treating it. Moms can sit and observe their kids' behavior while doing nothing about treating or correcting it. This type of parental neglect couldn't be more detrimental, not to forget self-perpetuating. And it could be preventable.

Takeaway Action Thought: While not all parent/child relational messes are avoidable, many of them are preventable.

Weight-Bearing Exercises

Women are experts at cleaning up other people's messes. It comes naturally, that nurturing bent to help someone get through a tough time, overcome a difficulty, or walk alongside in friendly fashion. When it comes to taking care of their young adult children, roles necessarily shift, and women can no longer rely on their "what's best for you" mom-mode. Still, armed with facts, moms can continue to be the go-to person when their kids have questions, concerns, or just aren't sure. Because their kids will come to them for advice, moms need to know some of the mistakes made most often in health-related issues. See below for some of the areas mostly commonly taken for granted.

∾ **Fact:** Children, teens, and young adults live for the moment. From their standpoint, today is all that matters; tomorrow is too far away. As a result, they seldom think about what they do today and how it will affect them tomorrow or next month or even in years to come. Young people have little awareness that today's choices can have profound effects on their health as an adult.

∾ **Statistics:** According to the Center for Disease Control and Prevention (CDC), 16 percent of today's children ages six to nineteen are overweight. This percentage represents nine million children. The number has tripled since 1980. The obese child is at risk for numerous health problems. These include diabetes, coronary artery disease, asthma, hypertension, and sleep apnea.

∾ **Prevention:** Experts agree that inactivity and poor eating habits contribute to obesity. National guidelines recommend 150 minutes of physical activity each week for elementary children and 225 minutes for older children. Most children do not meet this modest level of physical activity on a weekly basis.

≁ **Consequences:** It is important for parents to ensure that their children, teens, and young adults eat a healthy, balanced diet and exercise regularly. The CDC reports that 80 percent of children ten to fifteen years old who are obese become obese adults. Clearly, it is vital for parents to set the bar early on for a healthy weight and activity level, as failure to do so will likely carry a lifetime of obesity-related problems.

My child, listen closely to my teachings and learn common sense.
Proverbs 4:1 CEV

28

🙠 RELATIONSHIPS 🙡
Meeting Practical Needs
Up Close and From Afar

> Our openness, *when fitting*, makes us a magnet
> for the people around us who are longing for
> just one person in their lives to be "real," to
> listen to their story without raising an eyebrow,
> to let them weep without providing advice.
> Carol Kent in *A New Kind of Normal*

Whether we're keeping company with someone living close by or keeping up a long-distance relationship, real friends have each other's backs. It never matters how long it's been since we've seen a person (in person); people who care about one another don't let time, miles, or busyness get in the way. Friends carve out precious moments for staying in touch and keeping communication lines open. They know what each other needs most and supply it.

In this age in which so many individuals have adopted a transient lifestyle, here a few years, there a few (or fewer), enjoying real intimacy with people can be difficult. It's hard to be up front with friends even when they know you have their backs. Maybe hardest of all is the willingness (when fitting) to be honest about who we are, how we've failed, and where we're struggling right now. It's much easier to keep our conversation closed, confined, and casual. But keeping those we trust and who trust us at a comfortable distance feels strangely repellant, and it should. Wherever self-protective walls are fitted tightly in place, feelings of mistrust and hesitation will get in the way of what we all need most from our friends: truth and trust and help.

Physical distance notwithstanding, people have a hard time coming clean with who they are, no matter if it's with the person sitting next to them or a friend they see only via their computer screen. Interestingly, our society encourages the casual intimate encounter that leaves a person feeling more alone than ever, for there is no such animal as genuine instant intimacy.

Carol Kent, whose only son was sentenced to life imprisonment, recalls bolstering herself against people's intrusive comments and thinking, "My pain is none of your business." Later on, Kent slowly recognized that when she risked the willingness to be transparent with her doubts, hurts, and grief, this open-heartedness provided hope to others. Kent shares, "The first step—being honest with even one person about the imperfect choices or situations of our lives—is the most challenging. Fear taunts: *People will reject you and make you feel like a flawed person.* Faith says: *Take the risk. Be real. Allow God to use the broken places of your past to give hope to someone else.*"

And so real friends do the fitting thing: they really talk. They tell. They listen. They do it with words, or not. And somewhere in the midst of all the talking, telling, and listening . . . friends who share fare better than do those who refuse to be real.

Takeaway Action Thought: The formula for any well-fitting and lasting friendship is to take the straightest route to truth, trust, and help, no shortcuts allowed.

Weight-Bearing Exercises

Given the way families are changing, expanding, and moving around, there's a fair chance that we women will find ourselves having to lend a hand to those we love long distance. This scenario may not feel so daunting when family members are still reasonably fit and mostly able care for themselves, but what happens when the unexpected or the unplanned occurs? What may surprise many women is that while there are some resources available for taking care of loved ones long distance, it is important to know the accessibility factor has its limitations.

♋ **Detours:** Those who want to access effective, comprehensive care for family members living far away would be surprised to learn that there are no universal organizations set up to deal with ongoing long-term caregiving issues. Though there are agencies for elder abuse and related protective services, individuals will have to do their own legwork to find assistance city by city.

♋ **Long way around:** While there isn't a one-stop agency for every care-need scenario, families can find temporary assistance on a piecemeal basis. If a family member is in the hospital for any reason, address any questions and concerns to the staff social worker. These in-house representatives will be the most familiar with all local agencies available and can explain what types of services are offered and covered by various insurance or state-funded plans. Another potential bump is that most benefits are covered only for a few short weeks.

♋ **Shortest route:** If your family member lives far away and is in need of help, your best option is to go directly to the source. In the long run, you'll save time and possibly avoid catastrophe if you visit your loved one's home, familiarize yourself with the surroundings, and become acquainted with the community and those resources available to them.

❧❧❧❧

A friend loves at all times, and a brother is born for adversity.
Proverbs 17:17

29

ॐ HOUSE & HOME ॐ
Setting Boundaries That Make Everyone Feel Safe

> When we are in deep trouble we long to see
> some rescuer appear . . . Suddenly, decisively,
> kindness appears. And it is not the kindness
> of soft words or a gentle smile but a strong
> act of intervention, a mighty deliverance.
> Mel Lawrenz in *Patterns*

Where we live, how we shelter ourselves, and what our dwelling place looks like says a lot about us. Some assumptions may be true, others not. Whether we like the structure of our homes or make do with the resources we're given says something too. Are we content with the present condition of our home? Or do we catch ourselves eyeing that which appears newer, maintenance-free, and all-around more appealing than ours? How well do we care for and tend to that entrusted to us?

Whatever our inclination about housing and homes and the purposes these dwellings serve beyond protecting us from the elements, it must be remembered that how we live within our four walls matters. Anyone can dress up a house and make it look attractive to onlookers, but what counts is what happens on the inside, the side no one else sees.

Have you ever walked into a home that was beautiful on the outside but was falling apart on the inside? People feel unsettled, anxious, and confused when the outside and inside don't match. Something's wrong with this picture.

Like it or not, every family sets boundaries for themselves, and we're not talking the brick and mortar or the white picket fence. Rather, inside our home and around its periphery, people live by an unseen code that determines who gets in and who stays out. There's also a set pattern to the ways and means of our in-house interactions. Boundaries are there, and each one is set in something stronger than stone.

Our home life is indeed telling, as are our expectations for those living within our homes. For everyone creates certain lines that won't be crossed, and all individuals set specific boundaries around themselves that set limits even on those closest to them. It's safer that way, but not always so healthy. Boundaries are good only when they serve their purpose of offering protection, provision, and room to grow.

For individuals to thrive within the setting of hearth and home, some lines shouldn't be crossed. Disrespect, disregard, discomfort, discouragement are a few. Whenever our dwellings house these unattractive detractors, it is because of neglect, and where there is neglect, the value of the home and its occupants drops markedly.

No conscientious homeowner allows potentially harmful substances to infiltrate or devalue her house. But, do we permit it from the inside out due to simple neglect? Do we aggressively protect our borders by making sure every person is treated with respect and heartfelt regard and realizes the comfort of an encouraging word? It is always easier to work at keeping households in good repair than it is to tear down and rebuild after it has fallen into disheveled disarray. Lawrenz reminds us that homeowners everywhere decide daily how to protect their interests. Writes the author, "Kindness is a choice, not a temperament." Would that all who find themselves within our borders feel protected and provided for, and may the experience always be a pleasant one.

Takeaway Action Thought: Every kitchen should display the motto "Protection, provision, and room to grow," and no family member should travel far from it.

Weight-Bearing Exercises

Setting boundaries and feeling safe and secure within one's home is every woman's reasonable expectation. Sure, women may have to attempt one or another redo or makeovers before finding the right fit for themselves, but most are pretty confident that their homes are safe havens. But venture beyond the borders of the home routine, and the world outside can feel frightening, uncertain, and unpredictable. Even when women leave their familiar surroundings for something as pleasurable as a vacation, it can feel risky. Many choices seem a bit chancy, but taking some simple precautions and knowing your options helps alleviate the majority of pre-travel jitters. Be prepared before, during, and after you travel.

Before You Go

- Make a list of all medications and known allergies.
- Include your primary care physician and pharmacy phone numbers.
- Keep all medications packed in your carry-on, not in checked luggage.

꙰ If traveling for an extended time, bring a refill for all prescriptions.

During Travel

꙰ If you or a family member becomes ill, contact the hotel concierge or someone you know locally to find out where to go for medical care. A referral increases the odds of getting optimal treatment. Don't simply go to the nearest or most convenient clinic or urgent care facility.

Special Considerations

꙰ Those individuals prone to illness should consider buying travel health insurance before leaving.

꙰ Medical evacuation insurance is particularly helpful for overseas travel and can be purchased for a reasonable fee.

꙰ Refer to www.cdc.gov/travel site for specific information or warnings regarding the country you intend to visit.

Final word

꙰ Despite what we read in the news, the United States does have the best medical care in the world. So, given the option, do your best to get home to be treated. The old saying, "There is no place like home," truly applies to health care.

ꙅꙅꙅꙅ

The boundary lines have fallen for me in pleasant places.
Psalm 16:6

30

☙ TIME ❧
No Time Like the Present
to Change

I have little hope for a future brought about only
or primarily by human endeavors and initiatives.
I have great hope for a future brought about
by a God who pulls us forward by surprises
and spurts, ambushing us with so-beautifuls
and blessing the best out of our worst.
Leonard Sweet in *So Beautiful*

Time is such a nebulous factor, one that both commands us and paradoxically submits to our whims in equal measure. We either have too much of it, as when we're left waiting for some important (to us) event to transpire. Or, we have far too little of it, as we rush headlong through each task only to get through the next one and then the next. Time, either way you look at it, is laborious. It wears us out, frays our tempers, and tempts us to take matters into our own hands. Time at its taskmaster best can bring out the worst in us. Time is not easily mastered.

Time . . . though each of us is given the same amount of it, some of us are better managers than others. Why is it that a few individuals seem to breeze through their hours and days accomplishing only a fraction of what they might have planned (if they planned at all), and it doesn't bother them one iota? Others, those more conscientious types, take every item on their to-do list and do not, cannot, will not rest until every entry is completed. (This is done with a vengeance, mind you.) Could it be even the super-responsible among us inwardly know there's something more important than just getting stuff done and we're angry about it, because we know it's true and still aren't willing to give the thought of changing (ourselves, that is) the time of day? Sometimes knowledge without the courage to head in a different direction is a like incessant ticking of the nearest timepiece.

Better late than never, sometimes it is best to call a time out. Give it a rest. Stop and sit down. Close your eyes. Be silent. Be still. Then, take note. Begin to notice movements and moments and steps and gestures. Miss nothing. Pay attention to everything.

When we're unable to stop long enough for even this simple exercise, it should leave us wondering what's at stake here. Certainly, there's more going on than running headlong through the day only to get things done. When we're consumed by merely producing, we're missing so much more, and this much more is where real life is going on. Our excuse is always the same: there will be time enough for that later on . . . when the work slows down, when the kids are older, when my parents don't need my help, when my health gets better, when the worst is over. And when, exactly, will that be?

In case we didn't notice, there's a never-ending list of "when"s waiting one after the other that keep moving up on our endless to-do list of excuses. But if we're honest, and this is the best news ever . . . there's no time like the present. This precise moment is all we have; there's no getting it back once we've spent it or squandered it, more likely, by being busy, busy, busy people making our grand plans, believing we're doing everything we can to achieve our best, when all this activity might be the worst choice we make. Eventually, every one of us needs to take to task our assumptions about life and time and how we spend them both. There's no telling what tomorrow may bring.

Takeaway Action Thought: There's no time to lose, literally, so do an about face and stop. Refuse to move forward again without a focused action plan.

Weight-Bearing Exercises

As the pace of our lives gets increasingly faster, one season meshes into the next, one year into another, and before we realize it, decades have passed. It's especially true of women, who pass key milestones in life but are so pre-occupied by busyness that we forget the importance of self-care. So, the question becomes, Is it ever too late to begin taking better care of yourself? Are there ways every woman can make up for lost time? If so, what are they, and how can women quickly implement such practices to give the most benefit in the shortest amount of time? What can women do to reverse the aging process? Several lifestyle changes can result in improved health and positively affect the aging process. They're simple as 1, 2, 3 . . .

    ℞ **One:** Weight loss is one of the most significant ways to peel off the years. Not only will you obtain the cosmetic benefits of weight loss, but also you will receive many physical benefits. These include less stress on your joints and back, reduced risk of diabetes, improvement in blood pressure, increased mobility, and better sleep. **Focus point for change:** Concentrate on lowering fat and sugar intake for fastest results.

🙠 **Two:** Get seven to eight hours of sleep a night. Caution: too much sleep can have an adverse effect on overall health. **Focus point for change:** Clock in your nighttime sleep hours, but do not nap excessively during the day. Researchers from the California Pacific Medical Center Research Institute found that elderly white women who took a daily siesta were 44 percent more likely to die from any cause, 58 percent more prone to dying from heart problems, and nearly 60 percent more likely to die from non-cardiovascular or non-cancer causes. Those who napped fewer than three hours a week showed no increased chance of death.

🙠 **Three:** Address your stress, as it is one of the biggest factors in premature aging. Stress causes the brain to produce chemicals that directly affect health negatively. **Focus point for change:** Exercise several times a week to add muscle mass and strength and gain improved cardiovascular health. A study of 9611 adults in *Medicine and Science in Sports and Exercise* showed that those who were regularly active in their fifties and early sixties were about 35 percent less likely to die in the next eight years than those who were sedentary.

ربربربرب
Trust in God at all times.
Psalm 62:8

❧ CONCLUSION ❧

Twice during the last few years, I was given the opportunity to travel overseas with a close friend. On both of these occasions, we were transported out of everything familiar to us, by our own choice. We traveled in a country where English wasn't the primary language, so we worked hard and creatively to be understood and to get where we needed to go. Our accommodations were in some ways wonderful, in other ways quite uncomfortable to us. Even the food we ate was different, and we had to learn to ask for precisely what we wanted.

As we learned how to successfully traverse unknown territory together, it strengthened the bond of friendship between us. Neither of us will ever forget the wonder and beauty of discovery and how amazingly similar people are over the world. We laughed often, were sad a few times, and contemplated life's ironies at just about every turn. It was good for me; it was good for my friend; it was good for our friendship. But, as wonderful as these trips were, we both knew it would have been easier to stay at home. Travel, especially overseas travel, takes some planning, some forethought, some careful consideration. It also requires an investment of time, money, and no small measure of courage as we move out of what is comfortable to us and leave behind people we care about. It's interesting how similar traveling is to life's journey.

As we've discovered through the stories and life scenarios presented in this book, women constantly face challenges unfamiliar or uncomfortable to us. Sometimes we're hit with something that blindsides us, and we look around wondering what to do next. At other times even the smallest event triggers a surprisingly deeply felt reaction. Whether we're in the midst of a hard situation that requires decisive action on our part or one that we're wrestling through internally, women have choices to make. We'll feel stretched by these choices far beyond what we believe we can handle. They'll move us into situations that will feel unfriendly and maybe even hostile; and these decisions will force us to look at ourselves more honestly.

In real life, we'll face countless barriers, and they'll present themselves in multifaceted forms, but we can't let these unknown or unfamiliar obstacles stop us. Just as my friend and I found out when we were stuck in a foreign city looking for our hotel, sort of lost, hungry, tired, and cold . . . and it was raining . . . we kept asking for directions, kept asking for help, kept on walking until we found our way. It wasn't fun, it wasn't easy, and it sure didn't feel like a vacation, but it was worth it, and when we consider what we would have missed if we had turned back . . . it would have been regrettable.

Looking back, neither of us would ever have opted out of those trips, traveling hardships and all, because there were treasures we found along the way that we wouldn't have gained without taking those first steps into the unknown. And isn't that the message for all of us? We don't know what's around the next corner, but we do what we can to be as best prepared as we can. As Anne Lamott writes, everyone in this life needs a generous share of *Traveling Mercies,* and women can locate them through the face of a friend, a timely word of encouragement, or a strong grip of a comforting hand. May we all find grace and mercy in abundance to fit us for today's travels, no matter where they take us.

❧ WORKS CITED ❧

1. Carolyn Custis James, *The Gospel of Ruth: Loving God Enough to Break the Rules* (Grand Rapids, Mich.: Zondervan, 2008), 92.
2. Hippocrates; for classical and modern versions of the oath, see www.pbs.org/wgbh/nova/doctors/oath.
3. Edward T. Welch, *Running Scared: Fear, Worry, and the God of Rest* (Greensboro, N.C.: New Growth, 2007), 25.
4. Sharon Marshall with Jeff Johnson, *Take My Hand: Guiding Your Child Through Grief* (Grand Rapids, Mich.: Zondervan, 2001), 39, 98.
5. Carolyn Custis James, *When Life and Beliefs Collide* (Grand Rapids, Mich.: Zondervan, 2001), 56, 64, 229.
6. Edward T. Welch, *Depression: A Stubborn Darkness* (Winston-Salem, N.C.: Punch), 141, 214.
7. Paula Rinehart, *Better Than My Dreams: Finding What You Long for Where You Might Not Think to Look* (Nashville: Nelson, 2007), 93.
8. Gregory Floyd, *A Grief Unveiled: One Father's Journey Through the Death of a Child* (Brewster, Mass.: Paraclete, 1999), 28.
9. *Merriam Webster Collegiate Dictionary,* 10th ed. (Springfield, Mass.: Merriam-Webster, 1994), s.v.
10. Carolyn Custis James, *The Gospel of Ruth: Loving God Enough to Break the Rules* (Grand Rapids, Mich.: Zondervan, 2008), 115, 193.

11. Will Samson, *Enough: Contentment in an Age of Excess* (Colorado Springs, Colo.: David C. Cook, 2009), 100, 101.
12. Lauren Winner, *Mudhouse Sabbath* (Brewster, Mass.: Paraclete, 2003), 112.
13. Paula Rinehart, *Strong Women, Soft Hearts* (Nashville: Nelson, 2001), 79.
14. Nancy Guthrie, *Holding On to Hope* (Wheaton, Ill.: Tyndale, 2002), 10, 12.
15. John Ortberg, *Faith & Doubt* (Grand Rapids, Mich.: Zondervan, 2008), 11, 139.
16. Paula Rinehart, *Strong Women, Soft Hearts* (Nashville: Nelson, 2001), 167, 168.
17. Vinita Hampton Wright, *The Soul Tells a Story* (Downers Grove, Ill.: InterVarsity Press, 2005), 152.
18. Gary Chapman, *Love as a Way of Life* (Colorado Springs, Colo.: WaterBrook, 2008), 122.
19. Paul David Tripp, *War of Words* (Phillipsburg, N.J.: P&R, 2000), 15, 58.
20. John Ortberg, *When the Game Is Over It All Goes Back in the Box* (Grand Rapids, Mich.: Zondervan, 2007), 196, 197.
21. John Ortberg, *When the Game Is Over It All Goes Back in the Box* (Grand Rapids, Mich.: Zondervan, 2007), 97.
22. Sarah Zacharias Davis, *The Friends We Keep* (Colorado Springs, Colo.: WaterBrook, 2009), 67, 150.
23. Leonard Sweet, *So Beautiful* (Colorado Springs, Colo: David C. Cook, 2009), 248–49.
24. David H. McKinley, *The Search for Satisfaction: Looking for Something New under the Sun* (Nashville: W Publishing Group, 2006), 67.
25. Carolyn Custis James, *Lost Women of the Bible* (Grand Rapids, Mich.: Zondervan, 2005), 98; Larry Julian, *God Is My Coach* (New York: Center Street, 2009), 129.
26. C. S. Lewis, *A Grief Observed* (San Francisco: HarperSanFrancisco, 1961), 452; Sister Wendy Beckett, *Meditations on Silence* (New York: Dorling Kindersley, 1995), 36.

27. Richard L. Ganz, *The Secret of Self-Control* (Wheaton, Ill.: Crossway, 1998), 68, 88.
28. Philip Yancey, *Rumors of Another World* (Grand Rapids, Mich.: Zondervan, 2003), 157.
29. Carol Kent, *A New Kind of Normal: Hope-Filled Choices When Life Turns Upside Down* (Nashville: Nelson, 2007), 115, 116.
30. Mel Lawrenz, *Patterns: Ways to Develop a God-Filled Life* (Grand Rapids, Mich.: Zondervan, 2003), 68, 69.
31. Leonard Sweet, *So Beautiful* (Colorado Springs, Colo.: David C. Cook, 2009), 50.

About the Authors . . .

Michele Howe and Dr. Christopher A. Foetisch write lifestyle and general health columns for bizymoms.com and for *The Buzz Book*, a quarterly Northwest Ohio glossy magazine with a distribution of over 25,000 readers. They have collaborated on numerous women's health articles for print and online general readership publications as well.

Michele is the author of ten books for women and has published over 1,200 articles, reviews, and curriculum for more than 100 different publications. She is also a reviewer for *Publishers Weekly, Aspiring Retail*, FaithfulReader.com, TeenReads.com, KidsRead.com, and *ForeWord Magazine*. Her articles and reviews have been published in *FIRST for Women, Good Housekeeping, Redbook*, SheKnows, BettyConfidential, *Prevention, HelloWorld, Christianity Today, Discipleship Journal, Midwest Living, Christian Single, Parent Life, Virtue, Single Parent Family, Women of Faith, Called Magazine*, and *Focus on the Family*.

Dr. Foetisch is a board certified orthopedic surgeon who specializes in sports medicine. Widely published, Dr. Foetisch's credits include articles in the *American Journal of Orthopedics, Current Opinion in Orthopaedics, Sports Medicine,* and *Arthroscopy Review*. He has also acted as expert consultant for numerous community and national trade publications on the following women's health topics: midlife depression; lifestyle habits for optimal health; traveling tips for staying well; pre- and post-op considerations; and planning tips for caregivers.